WHERE THE WORLD ENDS

Geraldine McCaughrean

OXFORD
UNIVERSITY PRESS

OXFORD
UNIVERSITY PRESS

Great Clarendon Street, Oxford, OX2 6DP,
United Kingdom

Oxford University Press is a department of the University of Oxford.
It furthers the University's objective of excellence in research, scholarship,
and education by publishing worldwide. Oxford is a registered trade mark
of Oxford University Press in the UK and in certain other countries

Copyright © Geraldine McCaughrean 2017,
published by Usborne Publishing Ltd

The moral rights of the author have been asserted.

This educational edition first published in 2018.

All rights reserved. No part of this publication may be reproduced, stored
in a retrieval system, or transmitted, in any form or by any means,
without the prior permission in writing of Oxford University Press, or
as expressly permitted by law, by licence or under terms agreed with
the appropriate reprographics rights organization. Enquiries concerning
reproduction outside the scope of the above should be sent to the
Rights Department, Oxford University Press, at the address above.

You must not circulate this work in any other form
and you must impose this same condition on any acquirer

British Library Cataloguing in Publication Data
Data available

ISBN 978-0-19-842614-1

1 3 5 7 9 10 8 6 4 2

Typeset by Thomson

Printed in China by Golden Cup

Acknowledgements
Cover: Chris Gomersall/Alamy Stock Photo **p8-9:** Map by Ian McNee ©
Usborne Publishing Ltd, 2017

For Ailsa and Andy,
who introduced me to Kilda.

Contents

St Kilda 1727: A Map

1	Crossing Over	1
2	King Gannet	8
3	Two months earlier on Hirta	16
4	A Lateness	22
5	Doubts and Fears	41
6	Confessions	58
7	Miracles	76
8	Outcast	86
9	The Keepers	101
10	A Welcome Return	117
11	King Saul's Trews	126
12	The Crossing	131
13	Words and Silence	145
14	Haunted	155
15	Light	168
16	Storm	183
17	Rite	199
18	Spring Fever	211
19	Monsters	222
20	Witch Hunt	233

| 21 | The White Ship | 242 |
| 22 | Music and Love | 258 |

Afterword
Birds of St Kilda
Glossary

ST KILDA, 1727

LEWIS

ST KILDA

HARRIS

SKYE

SCOTLAND

SOAY

GLEN BAY

CONACHAIR

GLEN MOR

MULLACH MOR

VILLAGE BAY

OISEVAL HILL

MULLACH SGAR

RUAIVAL

HIRTA

DUN

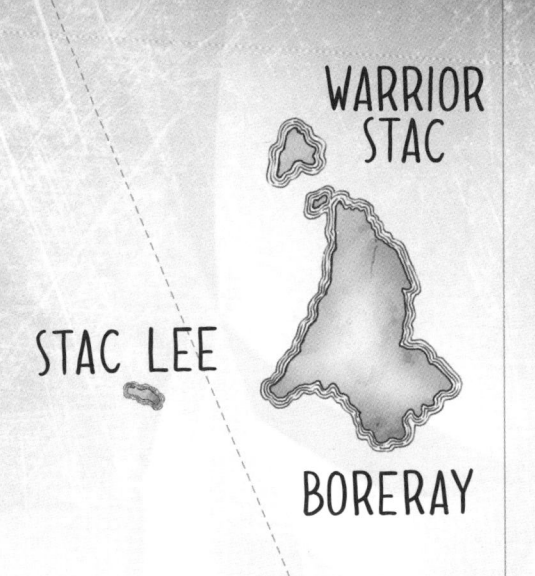

ST KILDA ARCHIPELAGO

WARRIOR STAC

STAC LEE

BORERAY

ATLANTIC OCEAN

1

Crossing Over

His mother gave him a new pair of socks, a puffin to eat on the voyage and a kiss on the cheek. "God will keep you safe, Quilliam, but he'll not keep you clean. You must do that for yourself." Happily, she did not try to hug him close.

He shook hands with his father, who remarked, quite amicably, "The floor needs digging out. You can give me a hand when you get back." Then Quill walked down to the boat. His parents followed on behind, of course, but the goodbyes were done and out of the way. Besides, he would be back in a week or three. They were only going out to one of the stacs to harvest the summer plenty: bird-meat, eggs, feathers, oil…

It was a blade-sharp August day, the sea burned black by the sun's brightness. And no, there were no omens hinting at trouble ahead. Hirta people notice such things. The clouds did not split open and let fall drops of blood: someone would have remembered that. No sinister bird settled on anyone's roof. A gull flew over and dropped its mess on Mr Cane – but that was nothing out of the ordinary. (Who wouldn't, if they could?) But no signs, no dread omens.

All the men and women of Hirta helped carry the boat down the beach. Three men and nine boys climbed aboard it, and a few people on shore raised their hands: not to wave, exactly, but to check that the wind had not swerved unkindly off course. Quill did not know if the maiden from the mainland was there, among the crowd – didn't look to see. To be seen looking would have had every other boy on the boat mocking him. So he didn't look. Well, maybe out of the corner of his eye. Once or twice.

The fathers and uncles, wives and aunts shoved them off. And no, the pebbles did not claw at the boat's keel. No lugworms squirmed out of their holes to lug it back ashore. Nothing out-of-the-ordinary shouted in their faces, *Don't go! Stay home!* It was a good launch.

Or maybe, if there were bad omens, Quilliam missed them, trying to glimpse Murdina one last time.

A journey out to the big stacs can take an age, even with a sail. Warrior Stac is so big that it looks close to, but there are four miles of open water to cross before you get there – water that folds itself into hills and valleys and doubles the distance. It was little Davie's first time out, and Quill could see the seasickness rising in him, as well as the fear. One day, if the years made him cruel, Quill might feel inclined to make fun of a first-timer and elbow him in the chest, as the bully Kenneth was doing now. But Quill remembered all too well his own first voyage – how he had expected every upward lurch of the bow to tumble the boat over, every trough between the waves to take them to the bottom. He remembered waves higher than a boat's gunwales; the spray soaking him to the skin. He remembered fretting about getting ashore without making a fool of himself, and then having to prove, day after day, that he could catch fowl as well as the rest; and having no bed to sleep on, and never a mother about for comfort at night... Poor little Davie: not the biggest birdie in the nest. And bless him, look, thought Quill, he has on his socks already, in place of his boots. All ready to climb.

Davie looked too green – in every sense of the word – to stand up to Kenneth and his bullying. But when he puked, he chose to do it in Kenneth's lap – an inspired revenge, thought Quill appreciatively.

They passed Stac Lee and got their first unhindered view of the place where they would be living for the next few weeks. John began to drum on the boards with his feet and the rest joined in, until Mr Cane (a reliable killjoy) told them to stop their noise or they would "wake every dead sailor from his resting place". The clatter died away, and Quill saw the youngest boys cast little superstitious glances over the side, in case dead sailors were a serious possibility.

Warrior Stac grows bigger the closer you get. You would swear it was pushing its way upwards – a rock whale pitching its whole bulk into the sky, covered in barnacles, aiming to swallow the moon. Nearby Boreray has big patches of green grass on it, but Warrior Stac is so big and so dark that all the fowl of the air since Creation haven't been able to stain it. It looms there, as black and fearful as one horn of the Devil himself. And it teems with birds.

To reach the landing place, the skipper had to round the base of the sea stac, passing right underneath the bulging shelf called "the Overhang" where a never-ending sleet of bird droppings pours down. The boat fell silent as each man and boy (except Kenneth) shut his mouth tight. "Look, look up there, Davie!" said Kenneth, pointing urgently upwards, but Davie had the wit not to fall for that one. No one looks up while he is under the Overhang. So only Kenneth caught a faceful.

For Quilliam, though, the Overhang was not the worst part of the voyage. That was the landing stage. The sea-swell slops up and over a bumpy jut of tilting rock. Getting ashore is a game you don't even try unless the wind is square-on from the north-east.

The old men back home talked about the stacs as if they were just larders, crammed with fowl put there by God expressly to feed the people on Hirta. But had *they* not been afraid? In their young days? When they went fowling on the Warrior? Had they never feared the jump from boat to cliff? The bow rises and falls so fast that the rock face seems to rush up and down in front of your eyes, the spray flies fit to blind you, and there's maybe a piece of kelp you'll land on, slippery as soap, and you'll lose your footing and go down between the boat and the rocks. There again, maybe Quill, like Davie, was just a scaredy-mouse.

Mr Don, barefoot and with a rope tied round his body (to fetch him back aboard if he fell) and the boat's mooring rope wrapped around his wrist, balanced precariously on the bow, and steeled himself for the jump. The Stac rose sheer in front of them, looking like the impregnable wall of a castle keep. And yet Domhnall Don made stepping ashore look easy. The fowling party formed a line in the boat: Mr Farriss and Mr Cane at the front, then Murdo, then Quilliam, then Kenneth, and so on in order of height: Calum, Lachlan, John, Euan, Niall and Davie. They had not only themselves to get ashore, but sacks, nets, coils of rope and wicks, baskets, clubs and a battered saddle…

A small, cold hand took a grip on Quill's wrist.

"Get back in line," he hissed, but Davie clung on, saying nothing, just looking from Quill to the cliff, Quill to the heaving waves, shaking his head. Quill threw his half-eaten puffin over the side, looped a coil of rope across his body, and when it came his turn, took a hold on the little lad's arm – so tight that Davie squealed – and jumped ashore with him. A great shining wave washed over the landing place a moment later, but Quill had hopped out of its reach by then. "Easy, see? ...Only *pick your feet up quicker next time!*" he called, as Davie scrambled away up the rock face, new socks all wet and flapping like a duck's flippers. It made Quill laugh to see them.

Looking back down at the boat, he could see the row of boys still aboard, left hands clenched white round their bundles, right hands just clenched, jaws set, all hoping to get ashore with their pride intact and without breaking any bones. (So maybe there was a touch of the scaredy-mouse in them all.)

Lachlan came past Quill, clambering ashore, nimble despite an armful of sacks and a bulky rope round his body. He was shabby as a moulting sheep, and twice as cheerful as he ever looked back home on Hirta. You would have thought he preferred the Stac to home. Why, thought Quill, when one wrong step, and the place will kill you?

But having thought it, he felt a sudden superstitious need *not* to think ill of the Stac. It did not mean anyone any harm. It was not a living thing, only a slab of rock in a big, cold ocean at the edge of the world.

Once the fowling party reached Lower Bothy, they stood about, drying in the wind, like cormorants, and watched the boat tacking away into the wind: homeward. Calum waved: the boatman was his father. Lachlan uttered a yelp of joy. Davie bit his lip. No going back now, till Calum's father returned to get them.

"Back soon," Quill told Davie, remembering that first time the sea had separated him from his mother.

No one wanted to be first inside the cave. Who knew what might be dead in there or – worse still – living? This close to the water, crabs and dying birds found their way in. Calling it "Bothy" made the place sound homely, like a hut or a cottage, when it was only really a dark, dank chink in the great wall of rock. Just twelve people, a heap of fowling nets, a cooking pot, six long ropes, an old saddle, egg baskets, bundles and boots. Cosy. In a few days they would move higher up the Stac, but in the meantime it was somewhere to dump the gear, and a good base for plundering the Overhang of its numberless gannets. So what if this was a stinky wet cave? Most of the time they would be outside, plucking riches from the kingdom of birds.

And every time a lad came fowling on the stacs, he went home less of a boy and more of a man.

(If he went home at all, that is.)

2

King Gannet

"Who wants to kill the King?" asked Mr Farriss.

It marked the beginning of their labours. No more housekeeping, clearing pebbles and bones and weed from their sleeping place. Today they were fowlers on a quest for gannets. "Who wants to be King?"

Every boy but Davie had his hand raised. The honour was huge.

"Quilliam, you have the years on you to be wise," said Mr Farriss.

Quill's heart expanded inside his chest...shrinking back down as Murdo pointed out: "I'm older!"

Mr Farriss looked at the two friends. After the Reverend Buchan had brought a library to Hirta, Farriss had been the first to use it. Now, he was the closest thing Hirta had to a schoolmaster, and fed the girls and boys of Hirta crumbs of book-knowledge whenever they were not needed to dig the rigs or climb the rocks.

He probably had favourites, but if he did, he never let it show. A scrupulously fair man. "Whichever is the smaller of you," he said.

Since there was no room to stand up straight in the Bothy, the two friends went outside to compare heights. It was no easier outside there, perched on a buckled cliff ledge. The two stood nose-to-nose. Both noses were running in the keen wind.

"I'm no' much fashed for it," said Murdo with a shrug. "You take it."

But, glancing down, Quill could see that Murdo's knees were bent in an attempt to make himself shorter.

"Me neither. You take it."

"Shall I?"

"Do."

But having honoured their friendship, nothing seemed to have been solved. So Murdo picked up a pebble and, palming it behind his back, held out both fists: *"Nicky-nicky-nack, which hand will ye tak?"*

And Quill chose the fist with the pebble in it.

Twin jets of joy and fear went through him: joy because now he might be able to tell his parents (casually, after a day or two at home), "Did I say? On the Stac, I was King Gannet." Fear, in case he failed.

A colony of gannets is a noisy, heaving mass of feathers, eggshells, bird lime and birds. For choice, it occupies the narrow ledges of sheer cliffs. But near the base of Warrior Stac, the Overhang bulges out like a fat man's belly. The slope of its surface is shallow – a perfect shelf for birds. The canny old ones walk over the backs of their neighbours, pairs sit contentedly side by side staring out to sea, the airborne home-comers crash-land on their fellow birds, crops full of fish.

A good place to start harvesting.

But high above any such colony perches a lookout bird: King Gannet. The crag he sits on is his watchtower; he is guarding the colony below. At the first sign of danger – blackbacks, eagles, fowlers – King Gannet sounds the alarm, and into the sky rises a blizzard of birds, shrieking and wheeling. Take out King Gannet and the way is open to wade in among the beaks and beating wings and reap a harvest of bird-meat.

And whoever kills the first lookout bird lays hands on its title, and becomes King Gannet for the duration of the trip.

The whole party crept as close as they dared without disturbing the flock. Mr Don was first to spot the lookout bird on the steep, black cliff that rose up sheer, behind the Overhang. King Gannet's throne was a finger of rock jutting upwards from a broad ledge. Quill changed his boots for climbing socks, warm and scratchy and thick-soled, but not so thick that he could not feel footholds in the cliff. He took off his father's over-large jacket – its sleeves came past his fingertips and it might flap in the wind – and entrusted it to Murdo. Then, from a point farther round the Stac, he started up the cliff face.

At first he climbed to impress the boys below with his skill. But there comes a point on any cliff when one mistake stops meaning a tumble and getting laughed at; it starts to mean broken bones, a broken skull, a bed in the graveyard. So, soon Quill was planning every move, holding still when the wind blustered, resting when cramp flickered in his calves. He took a diagonal route. To catch King Gannet unawares, he would have to creep across and up the cliff without being seen.

At one point, groping upwards for a handhold, he laid his palm down on an abandoned gull's egg, and the stale contents exploded, splattering down on his hair and trickling up his sleeve.

"I shall have you. I shall have you, Your Majesty," he whispered and, to throw off the humiliation of his eggy hair, imagined himself Odysseus climbing out of the Wooden Horse to capture the city of Troy.

Murdina had told him that story – a story from a different, faraway time and place. He had barely understood her talk of city walls and sandals and Greeks and Trojans: those were part of her mainland, educated world. But he had liked the story precisely *because*, like Murdina, it was strange and exciting. Murdina, for all she had only come to visit, had been genuinely interested to learn about Hirta, its people and customs and way of life. She had admired the courage of the fowlers – had quickly understood the dangers – had said how brave someone must be to go in among the slashing beaks and vast, bony wings… Suppose he could go home and tell her that he had conquered Birdy Troy? What would she say? What would be the expression on her face?

But when Quill was only halfway up the rock face, King Gannet gave a shriek and rose to his full height, wings wide and flapping – orchestrating chaos. Five thousand birds took off. Surely Quill had not…? Surely he had done nothing to…? Droppings rained down on him out of a thundercloud of rising birds. He held perfectly still, though the damage seemed done. The lookout bird teetered, hopped and took off, shrieking, *Intruder!*

Close by Quill's head, a clutch of puffins burst from a crevice in the cliff face, like little fireballs being lobbed at him. But Quilliam did not recoil. He did not flex a muscle, just clung steadfastly to the cliff – chiefly because he could not think what else to do. He turned his face downwards to shield it from puffin beaks…and so saw what had roused King Gannet.

A giant black bird with a white breast was wading through the colony. Even amid the big-winged gannets, it was immense. The great weight of its hooked beak seemed to unbalance it, because it set the tips of its stumpy little wings down, on rock or nest or gannet, to steady itself. When it looked up at him – and it did seem to look directly towards him – the big white circles round each eye were like a mask.

A garefowl. It must have mistakenly swum ashore below the wrong colony, and strayed into gannet territory while looking for its own kind. Being flightless, it could not extricate itself quickly, only clear a path with its massive beak and bulk. Delightedly, Quilliam watched the comical, tottering majesty of the "sea-witch", one minute standing waist-deep in gannets, the next standing, solitary and bewildered, as every last gannet took off. (Garefowl like to live shoulder-to-shoulder on land: they do not understand aloneness. There is no word, in their language, for "one garefowl".)

It alone had triggered the panic. It could take the blame, not Quill. And as soon as it had plodded its way onwards, on its big webbed feet, the gannets would finish circling, and settle back down.

Quilliam took the opportunity, while the sentinel bird was away from his perch, to clamber as far as the ledge that ran along behind the finger of rock. He inched along the ledge – even began to climb the pinnacle – but hearing the flapping of huge wings above him, froze to the stillness of a stone statue. Patiently, patiently, he waited, though his fingers lost their feeling and the summer flies droned around his eggy hands and hair.

The gannets circled, then sank down, a hundred at a time. King Gannet stood at full stretch, flapping his wings – all fussy self-importance. Then he settled back on to his throne, shoulders hunched, and peered down at the host returning to their roosts.

The climb – all that fingertip clinging on – had set Quill's hands shaking. He flexed his fingers until the spasms stopped. Then he felt about for a foothold wide enough, and launched himself upwards, onto a level with the King. In the same movement, he took hold of its wings and pinioned them behind its back, then freed one hand to wring its neck. A quick twist. A silent death. The gannets below noticed nothing.

"Fair. Fair," said Calum laconically afterwards.

Davie wanted to shake Quill's hand. All the other boys knew they could have done just as well, given the chance.

Mr Farriss said, with his little, crooked smile, "The King is dead: long live the King," and awarded Quill the title of "King Gannet" for the duration of their stay on the Stac.

Mr Cane said sourly, "The Lord smiteth the proud and bringeth down the mighty. Think on that, laddie."

Then they turned back to the task in hand – killing gannets, doing battle with beaks, battered by wings. But when Quill looked for Murdo, to get back his jacket, his friend had been sent on a separate expedition to catch fulmars. So he was obliged to go in among the gannets with only the thinness of his shirt. He barely cared. He felt invulnerable, clad in warm sunshine and the knowledge that he was a king.

They lit the evening fire using a pile of Murdo's fulmars. Fulmars burn better than wood, being an oily breed of bird. Then boys and men alike spent the evening cutting the stomachs out of dead gannets to serve as bottles for all the fulmar oil they were planning to take home. The Stac was full of riches – things the Owner would sell to city people who (unimaginably) had no birds of their own to feed and warm them, and must buy their feathers, oil and meat with real money.

Bedding down in the soft, welcome bigness of his father's jacket, Quilliam could not sleep, despite his weariness. He seemed to feel the whole weight of the Stac bearing down on their little cave. A single drop of water fell from the lip of the cave mouth, and he found himself waiting for the next to fall and the next and the next... Determined not to succumb to homesickness, he steered his thoughts, like a boat, towards pleasanter things. Murdina.

He fell asleep thinking of her, but his dreams were as chaotic as a colony of gannets. Through them blundered the great garefowl, white-masked like some holy highwayman. In his dream, her glossy black back was not soft with feathers at all, but a fall of young woman's hair, and from the ridged and hefty beak came songs Murdina had sung, about trees and lochs and love.

3

Two months earlier on Hirta

A bundle of clothes thrown ashore. If a wave had knocked the boat off-skew, the parcel might easily have fallen in the sea and been lost. But the skipper, Mr Gilmour, came over from Harris every couple of months, bringing supplies and mail. It was his particular genius: to fetch a boat nose-on to the rocks. No one else could do it. He knew every rocky flank of Hirta, and just how to time a throw ashore. He also had a good strong throwing arm, so the bundle of clothes bowled along the ground and came to rest among those waiting to welcome the boat's arrival.

The bundle contained the belongings of Old Iain, who had gone to Harris to visit his widowed sister, and died there. Not much to show for a life – a bundle of clothes – but some men die owning less. In due course, the villagers would share out the contents – make what use they could of the rags and remnants. The "Parliament" of village elders would decide who got the tobacco pouch, for instance. But for the time being the bundle was slung into the schoolroom; there were other parcels, crates and wallets of mail to be taken ashore.

"What did he die of?" asked Flora Martin.

"Of what did he die? A shortness of breath? An absence of life? What does any man die of?" asked the Minister, Reverend Buchan, grandly. "His race was run and now the Good Lord has taken him to His breast."

But something else came in on the boat, too. Murdina Galloway came. A mainlander. A niece of Mrs Farriss. She waited until the rise of the next wave and stepped ashore before the boat sank down again. Christ himself, walking over the sea, probably arrived with the same lack of fluster.

The prow bumped gently against the rocks. Many a boat had splintered planks against Hirta's cliffs: their wrecks had provided useful wood for doors and benches – there were no trees on Hirta. To anyone like Quill, who had never left home, a tree was a thing he could only struggle to imagine.

Murdina was much the same. Dark-haired, with winter-pale skin, she bore no resemblance to the women on Hirta. Their eyes were screwed into creases from peering into rain and mist or the sea's brightness. Hers were huge and round and peat-dark. Her hands were not rough or crab-crooked, but smooth and pale and long-fingered. She gestured with them. They talked, those hands – as did she.

Sometimes, on a windy day, everything indoors is calm and pleasant, then the door bursts open and in comes...the wind. It does not stay long. But it is...*disturbing.* Murdina disturbed Quilliam, and he did not generally welcome being disturbed. When life is harsh, everyday-ordinary is to be cherished. Excitements come from bad things – a baby born dead, a man falling from the rocks, the sheep breaking into your vegetable rig, a storm flattening the grain. The Minister spoke of "glories ineffable" awaiting them in Heaven: it was his favourite phrase, "glories ineffable", but since Quill had no idea what "ineffable" meant or what a "glory" consisted of, he had never quite got to grips with the idea. Everyday-ordinary was good enough for him. Then Murdina stepped off the boat, and Quill was full of glories ineffable. Feelings scrabbled about in him like a mouse inside an owl. She might be a niece of Mrs Farriss, come to help at the Minister's school, but she was *nothing* akin to anyone Quill had ever met.

There was the talking, for one thing. In sentences! Sentences as long as an anchor chain sometimes. They had him holding his breath to hear where they would end. Hirta folk are not great talkers. The women would gossip as they worked together at softening the tweed cloth or gutting fish. Hirta boys might chatter and giggle as they vied to see who could piss furthest. But generally Hirta mouths stayed closed. A wrong word can give offence. The cold wind can be painful on a troublesome tooth. Quill's mother liked to use the phrase "a thing said cannot be unsaid". And even Reverend Buchan (whose job it was to talk for *hours* in the church, on Sundays) made many a mention of "unclean lips" and "golden silence".

But Murdina talked to anyone and everyone, about everything. She even carried words around with her – there were never fewer than two books in her pockets. Mr Farriss's reading classes were anxious, troubling times for the children of the island, who strained and struggled to read down a page of words, like trapped sheep trying to get down a cliff. But then Murdina started helping out Mr Farriss with the lessons, and everything changed. Letters slotted together. Words came to life.

Losing patience with "A-for-apple", "B-for-box", "C-for-cat", she would launch into a story about Cats hiding Apples in Boxes in preparation for a war with Dogs when Eggs and Fish, Gugas, Hats and every other letter of the alphabet would get loaded into cannon and fired by the warring rivals... She told them stories. She read poetry to them from the books in her pockets.

She sang, too: lullabies and laments and love songs,
"The water is wide; I cannot cross o'er
And neither have I wings to fly..."

The Minister only really approved of hymns. He could just tolerate lullabies and working songs. Love songs sent shudders through him.

Murdina laughed, too, showing her perfect white teeth to the wind without the least fear of toothache. The Minister was disturbed by Murdina Galloway's laughter.

But not as disturbed as Quilliam.

Her laughter struck him like the clapper hitting a bell, and the reverberations shook their way through him. He was not sure what to do with the clamour. So one day, when there was a big, noisy sea running, he climbed to the top of Oiseval Hill and shouted it out of him, towards the horizon: *"Murdina Galloway! Murdina Galloway! Murdina!"*

The seagulls brought it back to him in their beaks: *"Murdina...Murdina..."* a thousand times repeated.

Of course, he could not tell anyone. She was a visitor. A mainlander. And a woman fully three years older then he. But when the wind blew her clothes hard against her body, Quill had no explanation for what he felt – unless it was the Minister's second favourite phrase: "sins of the flesh".

But she was only a visitor. A mainlander.

Shortly after the fowling party set sail for Warrior Stac, Mr Gilmour would arrive again from Harris with mail and timber, tools, blue dye, lamp chimneys, paper, books and tobacco. When he left, he would take with him the minister, Reverend Buchan, to report back on his missionary work. Murdina, too.

By the time the fowling party got back from the Stac, Murdina Galloway would be gone from Hirta. Quill would not see her again. The supply boat would carry her back to Harris. From Harris she would travel on to the mainland, where those unimaginable trees she spoke of would watch her comings and goings, day in and day out.

"I leaned my back up against an oak,
Thinking that he would shelter me…"

One day Quill had plucked up the courage and asked her to describe an oak tree to him, and she had said, "I shall do better, Quill. I shall grow one – just for you!" And she had drawn for him, with a sharp stone, in a patch of white sand, a big, big oak tree, and put leaves on its boughs – each one an imprint of her bare feet – and put pebble acorns in its branches. He had stared at it in wonder and disbelief for so long that he was late home for his dinner.

Next day, when he went back there, he had convinced himself the tree would still be there. He would be able to set his own bare feet in Murdina's leafy footprints. But of course the sea had erased it completely – so completely that he almost thought he had imagined it.

When he got home from the Stac, in three weeks' time, the sea would have carried Murdina herself away. Almost as if he had imagined her, too.

4

A Lateness

Within days of arriving on Warrior Stac, the fowlers moved house – from Lower to Midway Bothy, halfway up the Stac. It had no more home comforts than the Lower, but they could descend on ropes from up there and harvest birds from the cliffs. Also, it swallowed less spray when the sea was rough. They put the cooking pot outside to catch rainwater for drinking: it was simpler. The sacks were shared out to sleep on and under.

The older boys were quickest to grab a sleeping place. Though one patch of rock floor is no softer than another, the older ones knew that a flat space is better than one on a slope that seems all the time to be trying to roll you over. A ridge or a hole in the floor can leave a bruise by morning. A trickle of water from the roof can soak an entire boy overnight. Sleep at the back of the cave and there might be fewer draughts, but birds and mice have probably chosen to die there and rot. So, after the men had stated their claim, the boys who had been on trips before to the stacs grabbed their sleeping places within seconds, leaving the littler ones to fit in where they could. Davie stood by the cave-mouth, waiting patiently for someone to tell him where to sleep.

"You could hang 'em over a stone wall and they'd sleep deep, those wee ones," Quill remarked to Murdo, but still felt a pang of guilt at seeing the broken patch of rubble where Davie bedded down.

Visiting fowlers meaning to stay longer than a week would pile up boulders around the opening to keep out the wind. But no one wasted time on that now: the weather was mild, and the view too spectacular to block out. They could have seen all the way home to Hirta, if it were not for Stac Lee sticking up in between.

On the first Sunday in Midway Bothy, it was Col Cane who mustered everyone for prayers, and apologized to the Almighty for them working on the Sabbath. Quill could see the other men were annoyed that he should elect himself to the post of temporary minister. Euan, though, was always glad of a chance to say his prayers.

Euan: soulful, solemn little Euan whose voice had not broken yet, and who said colours had tastes, and that holy words were magic. Kenneth said that Euan was trying to get into Cane's good books by pretending to be a little saint. But the only good book Euan wanted to get into was the golden one where angels wrote your name if you were fit for Heaven.

Euan and John, Niall and Davie settled themselves at Mr Cane's feet, hoping for a Bible story or that their prayers would be answered if they could make it be like a proper Sunday. But the older boys sat at a distance, not convinced that Col Cane had any real magic to offer.

If Reverend Buchan, the actual minister of the kirk, was a chilly man, Cane was a bucket of cold water. He called himself "the Minister's Right Hand", though in fact he was only the sexton, employed to dig graves, tend the manse vegetable plot, mend the roof and clean the barn which served as a kirk. When the island's Owner presented the "kirk" with a ship's bell, Col Cane had made it his job to ring the bell, too, before services, summoning the villagers to worship. He thought it made him an important "officer of the kirk".

Quill's father whispered that Col Cane thought God was on the other end of the bell rope, and he pulled it to get the Almighty's attention. Quill's mother said she was thankful for ears, so that she could put her fingers in them. Quill suggested that if Mr Cane ever laughed, his own ears would fall off in surprise.

In short, Col Cane would not have been anyone's first choice as a stand-in minister.

They netted storm petrels that day, down at the water's edge. Like with fulmars, the trick was to keep the oil inside them, pinning their wings behind them before they could puke up the rust-red contents of their stomachs in a jet of terror. Bird oil was a cure for everything from toothache to lumbago, so people on the mainland (who could afford to get ill) paid a good price for it. Still, it was fiddly, greasy work emptying the little fulmar sacs into the big, rubbery gannet stomachs and knotting them closed. They were all glad when they could turn their attention in earnest to the most valuable birds off all – the gugas. The gannet chicks. Born in the spring, they had grown so big by August that they weighed more than their parents. Guga meat would fetch top prices on the mainland, and make for a sumptuous feast back on Hirta.

So, every day the older boys and men went out to catch guga. The babies sat, like fluffy dumplings, on narrow ledges of the steepest cliffs. It seemed extraordinary that they did not roll off and plummet flightless into the sea or bounce-bounce-bounce down the escarpments. To reach them, the older boys swung down the vertical cliffs, supporting their own weight on horsehair ropes looped under one thigh, and were pulled back up again by the men, the dead chicks hanging from their belts.

During the daytime, they caught gannets; during the evening they ate gannets. At night their dreams were shot through with puffins and fulmar, and riddled with gannets.

Murdo and Quilliam made a competition of the work, vying every day to see who could catch the most. They had been fowling together since they were first trusted to catch more birds than they scared away. They had passed muster on the same day, venturing out onto the terrifying Kissing Rock, high above a pounding ocean, bending to kiss the stone. It was proof they were competent enough to go fowling. Of course, once you were out fowling, you did not have actually to *kiss* the birds, just grab them by the neck. As Murdo pointed out, "If it were an easy test, you might go fowling next day and get killed, an' 'twould be a pitiful waste of all the porridge and clothes your ma and pa ha' given you since you were born." (Murdo thought a lot about the cost and value of things. Even people.)

Murdo's father had made and owned the finest rope on Hirta – plaited horsehair hand-sewn into a sheepskin sheath. One day it would belong to Murdo, bequeathed to him, as lords and gentlemen bequeath their houses and lands and swords to the first-born son. And one day Murdo would like as not pass it on to a son of his own.

Euan had already inherited his rope – his father had died in a fall – but he was not old enough yet to do rope work. Still he had brought it along: each rope taken on a trip earned a "wage" payable in birds or feathers, and Euan's mother needed such extras now her husband was gone.

So it was on Euan's rope that Quill found himself dangling, high above the sea, taking gugas with one hand, while supporting his own body weight with the other. Under one thigh and over the other, ran the rope – a soft, pale loop of beauty – rather like Euan, really.

A worn-out pony saddle battened to the rim of the cliff kept the rope from getting cut or worn on the sharp cliff edge. Davie, for some reason, gave himself the job each day of lugging this saddle from the Bothy to the cliff and watching Mr Farriss fix it in place. "It is safe now, Quilliam," Davie would say, nodding earnestly, then rush off in his socks to join the younger boys plucking birds.

There were upwards of eighty cleits on the Stac: little towers built of rocks, where the dead birds were stored to dry. A cleit keeps out all but the wind, and wind dries the birds inside almost as well as a smokehouse. Sitting with their backs to a cleit, little huddles of boys would pluck away at the birds they had caught, stripping off feathers until the tower and the ground and the boys and the air were all downy white. The younger ones crammed the feathers into sacks until, day by day, weightless fluff became as heavy as bags of stones. Thanks to them, some day soon, a rich mainlander would sleep on a feather mattress stuffed with down that smelled not only of birds, but the fish those birds had eaten and the sea that had held those fish.

The August dawns sliced their way cleanly through the horizon. The sunsets were feathery and pink. The brief nights were spark-filled with stars.

But working from dawn till dusk meant fifteen hours of fowling: climbing, plucking, strangling, netting, lugging, storing, rope-mending, bottling, "beachcombing" for firewood, egg-gathering, puffin-snaring and the wicking of petrels. By the time the sun was at its highest, boys were falling asleep whenever they sat down – on ledges and clifftops and scree slopes, and would have to be woken, for fear they turned over in their sleep and fell to their deaths – woken, too, to go back to work, gathering, snaring, plucking, storing…

Still, there was satisfaction to be had from the numbers of feather-filled sacks, the bursting cleits. Hard work plucked the hours and minutes out of the days, and the wind just blew them away. Soon they would be home on Hirta.

Three weeks and then a fourth.

The boat would come when it could. Tides and winds would decide. Perhaps Hirta's one and only boat had scraped its hull against rocks, or developed a patch of wood rot: some repair was needed. Maybe Calum's father had hurt himself and could not sail it. In that case, surely, Mr Gilmour would come instead, in the supply boat, since it must be time for another delivery of goods? Well, perhaps not. Perhaps there was no mail to deliver. Perhaps "Parliament" had not ordered any supplies.

Mr Cane marked two more Sundays with prayers and stout advice. Then another. The boys dared not gripe, but the job of work on Warrior Stac began to feel less of an honour and more of an ordeal. Even Mr Don – a stolid, implacable man – began to grunt and mutter to himself that he needed to get back to mending his roof while the weather was good. Mr Farriss wanted to get back to his wife and babes.

Quill stopped inventing reasons why Murdina Galloway might have stayed on in Hirta instead of going home: he was never going to see her again now, not ever. So he settled for wording imagined letters to her, dropping a mention here and there of the number of gugas he had taken, or about being King Gannet, and how much he missed her singing. In his imagination, Mr Farriss did not even have to help with the spelling.

In his imagination, Murdina wrote back.

A team of boys and men who can work a sea stac for four weeks can work it for longer. Of course they can. No one dies of sleeping on a rock floor. They had plenty of birds to eat, to light their cave and kindle their cooking fires. So what if they were dirtier now than their mothers would have liked? A little dirt helps keep you warm. They wanted to be going – were ready to get back to their dogs and ponies and sisters and (above all) the proper earth-dug toilets behind their house. But no one wanted to be the first to gripe – make himself sound puny. Only the sound of Davie crying softly after the last glimmer of the cooking fire blinked out kept Quill awake a while. That and the *drip drip drip* of water from the lip of the cave mouth.

The gugas fledged and turned into adult birds, shrinking to the size of ordinary gannets. The summer sea darkened.

"Why do they not come?" asked Calum, and everyone glared at him for saying out loud what they had been so scrupulously keeping to themselves. Calum had gouged open a hole everyone else had been trying to plug.

"There will be a good reason," said Domhnall Don.

"As soon as they can, they will come," said Mr Farriss.

"We are in God's hands," said Mr Cane, pompous as ever.

"What if it's pirates?" blurted Niall: the words rushed out of him as if brigands were after them.

The question lay unanswered. Niall never asked it a second time – not because it was ridiculous, but because the answer did not bear thinking of. Not in their lifetime, but within the memory of their grandparents, pirates *had* come to Hirta. They had ordered all the people into the kirk, then set the kirk alight. Stories like that, they're for adults at Halloween, not for boys far from home. Murdina would never have set such a story loose in a boy's head. Quill wondered what comforting thing she would have said instead. What would she…? What should he…?

"Like as not, they took the boat out fishing and scraped a rock and they had to go chasing after wood to mend her – such as the minister's gate – but the Parliament of Elders wouldna let them take that, so they hadta wait for some wood to wash up and then they hadna the right tools to fix the boat, because Mr Don is here, not there, and Mrs Don canna lay hands on his chisel, because maybe Mr Gilmour had a borrow of it and forgot to give it back and took it home to Harris when he sailed."

"Thank you, Quilliam," said Mr Farriss, and sincerely meant it, because it had taken the jitters out of the little ones and mesmerized the others.

"Quill has eyes for your niece, Mr Farriss," said Kenneth, snide and jeering. His lower teeth naturally overlapped the top ones so that his jaw was always jutted, belligerent-looking, like a hog.

There was a general sniggering, which mortified Quilliam and baffled little Davie. "What, the mainland maiden? Miss Galloway, d'you mean? But she's so black! And she has a big nose!"

"Like a garefowl?" said Niall and there was more laughter.

Mr Farriss scowled at Davie for his bad manners, but the boy was simply startled at Quill's idea of beauty.

Quill denied it, of course. He absolutely denied having eyes for anyone. But Kenneth went on wearing that glinting smirk of his. Kenneth picked up secrets wherever he went – little sharp things that might come in useful when he wanted to cut deep and give pain. So Quill did not argue about the size of Murdina's nose – which, in his opinion, was very like the nose the Queen of Sheba probably came fitted with. And he did not say that black hair could be every strand as beautiful as brown or red.

Conversation turned to "foreigners" in general. Whether from across the oceans, or in the devilish cities of Scotland, or on the big islands like Harris, Mr Cane declared them all "worldly" and "too much given over to making money and merriment". (How he knew this was anyone's guess, since he had never travelled farther afield than the sea stacs.)

"The Owner lives on Harris," said Domhnall Don solemly, and scowled at Cane.

No one spoke ill of the Owner of St Kilda. Like God, he never visited the isles in person – only sent his Steward once a year to collect the rent from his tenants. Like God, he was held in awe by everyone on Hirta. The very fact that he could *own* a whole archipelago of islands and stacs made him seem like the Creator Himself.

Col Cane blushed and blustered. "There may be some – like the Owner – who lead good lives," he conceded. Mr Don looked over at Mr Farriss and winked.

At least there was no more talk that evening of why the boat had not come to pick them up.

And a thing not talked about barely exists, does it?

"Have they forgotten us?" asked Davie as he helped Quill put the capping back on a cleit. The little stone tower was full to the very brim with birds now. The ones at the bottom must already be dry enough to sell. "Have they, Quilliam? Have they forgotten us? Must we live here for ever?"

"Away with you, ninny. 'Course not. They'll come tomorrow. Next day, maybe. Soon." Quill was weary of scouring about for explanations to soothe the fears of the littler boys. He was irritable – sick of being always in company. Everyone's temper was short.

Mr Farriss was indignant about the boys being "kept so long from their kin". Mr Cane intoning down his nose every five minutes, *"What cannot be altered must be endured"* made Mr Don writhe with annoyance.

Perhaps the blue-green men, shaped out of the sea's foam, had come ashore and kidnapped wives for themselves.

Perhaps lightning had struck.

Perhaps there was a war somewhere, and the Owner had sent all the men on Hirta to fight for Scotland.

No one believed a word – not even the people who made the suggestions.

Until little Euan spoke.

Mr Cane was leading prayers. The Bothy was lit with bird-lanterns, the rigid oily little bodies of dead storm petrels threaded through with tarry wicks and lit with

Cane's precious tinderbox. They burned as brightly as any beeswax candle in a French chandelier and would smoulder right down to their feet before they went out.

Quill had his eyes closed but was not praying. Rather than listen to the drone of Mr Cane's miserable voice, he was trying to conjure up the face of Murdina Galloway, for fear he'd forget it. Suddenly Euan, seated in a low corner of the cave, jumped up, then gave a cry. The cry was followed by a general gasp. Everyone had looked around to see him, hand raised to his head, fall face-first onto the floor. He lay like a dead thing. Mr Farriss scuttled over to him, bent double.

"He hit his head on the roof!" said Niall, aghast. "Is he dead?"

But Euan stirred, turned over and stared about him – not at the people, but at the cave walls, as if pictures were painted there that only he could see. "I know," he said.

"What do you know, boy?"

Blood trickled furtively out of Euan's hairline, like an unthinkable thought escaping into the open. "They are all gone up."

"Gone up where, boy? Who?"

Mr Cane made huffing noises at the interruption to his service.

"They have been taken up, do you see?" said Euan, blue eyes wide. "I seen it like a picture in my head: the End of the World, and everyone getting taken up to Heaven to be judged. But we were not seen, because we were in-the-rock, and now they're gone up and we are left behind." His high, musical voice was both awed and terrified.

No one laughed. Around them on every crevice of the rock walls, headless petrels burned, the wicks encircled by haloes of flame, as though a band of skinny little angels was peering down at them. They made it easy to believe the unbelievable.

God had decided to end the world. The Last Days had come. A golden trumpet had sounded and sent God's angels down to earth to fetch all the good people home to Heaven and pack off all the bad people to Hell. The angels had visited Hirta because it was big and green, and had houses on it. But they had never thought to look on the stacs, because the stacs were only lumps of rock sticking out of the sea – and who lives on a rock, apart from limpets and birds? Not people. Not men and boys sheltering in a rock crevice. So, by accident, the fowling party had been left behind in an empty world.

Niall, Davie and Lachlan ran outside into the near darkness of a rainy day and began shouting up at the sky. *"We are here! Look! We are here! Pull up! Pull up!"* It was the shout of fowlers who have finished a day's rope work: *Pull up! Pull up!* The pricking rain made their faces twitch.

The rest of the boys hesitated. "Is that right, Mr Cane?" asked half a dozen voices, because, for all he was a pompous and dismal man, Col Cane was the closest thing they had to a minister on the Stac. "Is Euan right?"

Cane did not answer at once and his expression was hard to read. He still seemed inclined to press on with the service that Euan's vision had interrupted. He did not like the boy, Euan, who showed a tendency to mysticism and prettiness which was none too Presbyterian. The noise of hysteria outside the cave made Cane pucker his bushy eyebrows. He wiped the corners of his mouth where spittle tended to cling. His eyes shot to and fro, without lighting on any one face, then he said: "Euan has the truth in him. I myself have been minded to think thus during my own contimpations. I kept silent fearing to cause upset among the younger ones. How-so-be-it…"

That ridiculous, pompous *"How-so-be-it…"* hung in the cave, lethal as the rumbling before a rockslide.

"How-so-be-it, this boy has been sent a vision, and we must swallow the fearful truth. Our Lord has gathered in His lambs and, being…*away from home* ourselves…we have been…for a short time…overlooked." Cane nailed home his argument: "Ask yourselves: what else can have happened?"

Mr Farriss and Mr Don plainly disagreed. Whenever Col Cane put on his sanctimonious voice and pretended to know the mind of God, they always rolled their eyes and growled. They were both devout, God-fearing men, but unlike Cane, they had children on Hirta and it would take more than the End of the World to make them forget it.

"If we can get across to Boreray," said Don, "we can signal home from there…" He said it every night, believing it the only route to rescue. But no one was listening. The boys were variously crying, calling for their mothers, asking questions or simply rocking on their haunches, arms over their heads. Quilliam, who had balanced fearlessly on many a cliff-ledge, suddenly knew what it was to be falling through fathom upon fathom of fear. His hearing was muffled, his eyesight shot through with colours. The End of the World? The End of…

A visiting boatman had once confided to him that drowning was not so very terrible. The secret was to stop struggling for air and take a single deep-water breath. So Quill breathed deeply now, and found the falling slowed; found himself suspended in a thick liquor of calm. "What do I do?" he said out loud. But the racket of the boys outside made it impossible to think of an answer. *Murdina, what do I do?* he asked, without letting the words escape his mouth.

He ducked out of the Bothy, and the cold air told him how feverishly hot his skin was. The hysterical boys were standing perilously close to the edge, their feet scuffing pebbles over the brink to fall all the way down to the sea. In their agitation, they were pushing and pulling at each other.

"We should make a signal! What d'ya say?" Quill said it again, louder, and again and again, until he had their attention. "Let's us make a signal – and keep it burning, so no one can forget we are here!" Davie unthinkingly took hold of Quill's hand, as he might have taken his father's. "Think on this," said Quill. "The angels must be working theirselves weary fetching home the good folk. All those countries to visit – all those cities! No ear to spare for listening. But when all's done and finished, our people will tell them soon enough: 'Hoi! You missed a few!'" Their eyes fastened on him with such intensity that he was embarrassed. Did they suppose that he really knew any more than they did? All he knew was that he had to get them away from the cliff edge. "Then the angels will clap their wings to their mouths 'n' groan 'n' haste on back here to find us!" (What kind of nonsense was he talking?) "'S'a long way from the mainland. Hard to find! You recall how Mr Farriss showed us a map once? Of the world? And Hirta was nowhere marked on it?" (What was he suggesting now? That God's angels were using inaccurate maps?) Why did the boys not laugh and tell him he was a fool? But no, they continued looking at him with such a desperate thirst for information that he carried on despite himself. He assured them that, one day soon, the angelic host would sail into sight or come galloping over the waves in chariots of gold, and that a signal fire was what was needed, to guide the boats (or chariots) through sea mist or night darkness, so that the angels would not pass straight by. It was simply a matter of staying safe until they arrived – taking care – because anyone dying right now might miss the coming of the angels to take them to Heaven.

Did he believe it himself?

Not for a moment. But as a diversion, it did the trick.

The boys abruptly noticed the closeness of the edge and moved away from it. Niall fastened the trailing laces of his boots. They waited for more instructions.

"Lachlan, go and ask Mr Cane if we can use the tinderbox," said Quill.

But Lachlan came back without it. "Mr Cane said I couldna be trusted. So I brought this." He opened his coat and revealed a little haloed, headless body sheltering inside his jacket: a petrel-candle, still burning. Col Cane was wrong: Lachlan could be trusted to do whatever was needed.

The four of them clambered as far as the nearest cleit and uncapped it. There were nets stored inside, and Quill said that those were too valuable to burn because they might still be needed. So they pressed on to the next cleit, one crammed with a mixture of gugas and puffins.

They made an excellent bonfire, those birds. Light and smoke streamed out through the gaps in the stonework and swirled around the boys' legs, lit their faces, made them sneeze.

"They will come now," said Davie solemnly. "The angels will see our fire and come."

"Soon," said Quilliam. "Quite soon. Possibly."

Did he believe it?

Not for one moment.

Where were the omens that would have foretold the end of all things? People on Hirta were continuously watching out for omens to tell them what the coming days might bring. They watched for soul birds, strange-shaped clouds, a ring around the moon, a shooting star... Surely God would have signalled that the world was over and done with? Where were the signs promised in the Bible: the blood-red moon, the beast with numbers on its forehead, the sea drying up? There would have been signs, surely. More than just the lack of a boat to fetch them home.

Smelling the smoke from the burning birds, he could think only of good food gone to waste. They might need every morsel if they were to stay on the Stac for... But he refused to finish that thought. It was unthinkable.

5

Doubts and Fears

Next morning, despite the world having possibly come to an end, another day's fowling began. Because what else was there to do? Quill was glad of it: the climb to new roosts would give him a chance to talk to Murdo on his own, and Murdo could always be relied on for wholesome good sense.

But John insisted on climbing alongside him, asking questions as if Quill (who had mastered the mystery of reading) might know the answer. "The angels – do they know a person's secrets without asking? And do they keep what they know to theirselves or spread it round Heaven until everybody knows it?" The red-cheeked, plump face was agitated and that quite altered it, because John was generally as placid as a pillow. (The only time Quill had ever seen him alarmed was when they had stood outside Niall's house together and listened to Niall's mother giving birth.)

"Secrets? What y'asking me for? Wasna me had the vision."

"I'm asking 'cos I thought *you* might have secrets," said John defensively. "'Bout the foreign lassie."

"Well I havena!" He tried to climb faster, so as to move ahead. But John had broad hips and bandy legs, so took a powerful long, lizardy stride up any rock face, and kept level.

"But if you *did* have a secret…"

Cornered, Quill sighed heavily and invented an answer: "Reckon they canna smell out a secret 'less it stinks o' badness," he suggested. "If it's a sweetish secret, they'll not be troubled." John paused to take this in, and Quill veered away in search of his friend.

But when Quill tracked him down, Murdo was shirking work to sit on a mucky ledge and throw rock chippings into the sea. He had wound himself in his father's rope and was equally entangled in some furious train of thought.

He kept talking about "shares" and his "due". "If we've to stay, we must each man have a cliff that's ours!" were his first words. "Am I not right? The slopes must be shared out, like at home. The youngest will get the easiest ones and we the worser, because we are older. So the birds we take must be ours, and not shared, right? I mean to mark every bird I take from now on. You must, too… An' I wants cleits of my own, to store mine in, so I can say, *These birds are mine – hold off yer paws!* And whose is the saddle now, would you say? Do we all own it? And who'll pay the ropes? Will the ropes get paid? Father's rope is mine now, so I'll be wanting the rope-money!" It was nonsense – gibberish, almost – but Quill could not break through the wall of words his friend was piling up around himself. Murdo kept slamming the heel of his hand against the rocks and practising his arguments: about how the Stac must be shared out fairly among them if they were going to live out their whole lives there.

"Our whole lives?" said Quill, glimpsing at last the image in his friend's head: a lifetime perched on a barren rocky pinnacle; nothing to eat but the summer birds; no one left living to rescue them; no one left to make life fair again. "Away! We'll be off here soon enough!"

"It's all very fine for you!" Murdo said, pushing him away ferociously. "You've *lived.* I never even got started. I wanted… I never even had a…"

A flicker of distant wings came out of the sun, impossible to identify thanks to the brightness. Murdo sat bolt upright.

"Someone will come," said Quilliam. "From Hirta, I mean."

"I know that," snapped Murdo, but his eyes were on the flutter of movement approaching along the sunbeams. "Euan is a fool. Euan was always a fool," said Murdo, but his quick glance begged Quill to see what he was seeing.

"What did you 'never have'?" Quill asked.

Large shapes, fast moving; wing beats so powerful they could be heard above the roar of the sea. Murdo lifted both hands from his precious rope, and raised them in the air – a gesture of welcome. Or surrender. The angels were truly coming for him!

"*Blackbacks!*" yelled Quill. "*Get down!*"

Then the blackbacked gulls were on them, mobbing and pecking and battering them with steely wings, aiming for their faces with vicious beaks. Quill and Murdo curled up in a single ball, shielding each other from the marauders shrieking in their ears. *Get off our stac!* the birds seemed to say. *Get back where you came from. These cliffs are ours!*

The attackers finally relented and roosted higher up, fluttering and muttering. Quill and Murdo uncoiled themselves and turned instantly away from one another, Murdo to conceal the fact that he was crying, Quill to be sure he did not see it. But he had felt the rage go out of his friend, and the hope, too. The precious rope spilling out of Murdo's lap made it look as if the blackbacks had torn the very guts out of him. In a way, they had: a flock of vicious birds is a poor substitute for a host of angels.

If even Murdo believed in the possibility of angels – thought the world had come to an end – perhaps Quill was the fool, after all, for doubting it. They had never disagreed on anything before.

"What did you never have?" he asked, as if their conversation had not been interrupted.

"A sweetheart, 'course," said Murdo.

Quill was mystified. "Nor me."

"But you love Miss Galloway."

Quill would have denied it, but he was intrigued to know: how did that constitute having a sweetheart? (Murdo had older sisters and knew more about such things. He had been able to tell Quill about the monthly mysteries of women, after all.) "Murdina didna love me back, man!"

"So?"

"So if you love a lassie, does that make her your sweetheart? D'you not have to – you know – have prospects?"

"Nah, man. Once you have her inside your head, that's like you've put a wall round a cow, so the cow canna wander off. She's your cow 'cos you built a wall round her."

For both of them, this revelation quite dispelled the pain and fear of the blackback attack. Murdo felt wiser for knowing something Quill did not, and Quill felt he had mastered a magic he never knew of before. Murdina Galloway might be far away in the mainland – possibly even farther away, in Heaven – but the woman in his head was still his captive. King Gannet had a sweetheart! "Could you not take a sweetheart yourself, so?" he suggested.

45

Murdo looked about him, spreading an empty pair of hands. *What, imprisoned on a spike of rock?* said those empty hands. *With eight other boys? After History has just ended?* What were the chances?

"Perhaps when you get to Heaven?" suggested Quill.

Murdo pulled a face. "I wanted to lie with a girl, not just look at her! Ye canna do that while you're standing about in Heaven singing hymns, and with all sorts looking on… And I d'na think we get to keep our bodies there, either. We are just wee spirity things, a-floatin'."

"Ah," said Quill, who had not thought so far ahead.

Euan did not go birding next day. Nor did Col Cane. They might not have been missed, but there was a blustering, snatchy wind blowing that might pluck a climber off his rope or a skinny boy off a rock face. So Domhnall Don decided they should turn to netting birds instead. Sent to fetch the net and the tinderbox, Quill and Murdo arrived to find the cleit where the net was stored was being turned into an altar. Col Cane had kept back Euan to help him decorate it. Here (Cane told them), he would be holding prayers every day, at dawn and dusk.

"Ay, but can we get to the net, Maister?" asked Murdo.

Euan pointed out that the bird-net had been used instead of an altar cloth and stuck through with sea pinks in place of embroidery. Much to Cane's annoyance Euan had spent all morning prettifying it. As the boys admired his handiwork, a particularly sharp gust of wind plucked the flowers out one by one and stripped the net bare again. Grudgingly, Mr Cane allowed them to lift the flat capstone and pull the net free…though he did not help with the lifting himself. Asked for the loan of his tinderbox, Cane again refused. "Do you have the fire-penny to pay me?" he asked me.

"Us, Maister? No, Maister."

"Then no, you canna have the tinderbox. If you've a need of light, then I shall bring light. I shall be 'Keeper of the Tinderbox' and when it is truly needed, I shall bestow it."

Murdo did not understand. "So…would you come now, then, Mr Cane? Mr Don wants a light. To draw out the puffins?"

"'Minister'," said Euan. "You must call him 'Minister Cane' now."

Again, Murdo and Quilliam looked at one another. They were ready to call Col Cane the King of Scotland if he would just loan them the tinderbox, but when the man still refused, they decided Cane would never be anything more than the village gravedigger as far as they were concerned.

The little cave for which Domhnall Don wanted the net was home to dozens of families of puffins. Puffins like crevices. Where there is peat and earth, they build burrows, but where there is only solid rock, they nest in crevices and cracks. Two fowlers would spread the net across the doorway, then those inside would light a flame in the middle of the cave. Lured from their hiding places by curiosity over the flickering light, the birds could be knocked out of the air with belts or sticks or bare hands.

Without a flame to attract them, the birds had to be dislodged by boys thwacking their jackets against the walls of the cave. Kenneth, armed with Mr Don's broad belt, stood in the centre of the cave and swung it at anything that came by him.

The first time he caught Calum a blow, it seemed like an accident. But when he caught John on the thigh and Murdo on the backside, the grin on his face made it plain he got more pleasure from hitting boys than birds.

"Stop that, Kenneth," said Murdo.

"Stop wha'?"

Puffins pelted them, too, their preposterous beaks hard as hammer heads as they hurtled out of the rock walls and collided with the fowlers. The men outside, holding the net, heard their yelps and blamed the puffins, so that Kenneth's reign of terror lasted until the nets in the doorway were so stuck with puffins that there was too little light to see by.

Secretly, Kenneth wanted to be thrashing angels out of the air, breaking their wings, bending their trumpets, punishing them for keeping him waiting. Whenever things went awry for Kenneth – disappointed, scared or thwarted him – he filled up with unmanageable temper. If, like a fulmar, he could have puked it out of his mouth it might have eased his rage. As it was, the bully had to settle for hurting puffins and children.

Naturally no one said anything of it to Mr Farriss or Mr Don: it is not the way of boys to run crying to their elders. But Lachlan must have been left with a greater loathing for Kenneth than the others. As the party scrambled home across the Stac, picked on by the bullying wind and burdened with a great netted ball of dead puffins, Lachlan clambered nimbly past ponderous, bulky Kenneth. He pointed to the bruise Kenneth's belt had left on his neck and pulled a sad mouth. "Shame. Never get up to Heaven now, Kenneth, will you? They dunna let your kind in." Those who heard it feared for Lachlan's safety, but Kenneth came to a sudden halt, and blocked the way of those behind him, and had to be told by Domhnall Don to shift himself. Lachlan was so much smaller and younger that Kenneth seemed unsure whether the boy was serious. Or perhaps Lachlan's jibe had pierced some painful part of Kenneth's soul.

It is not clever to be out alone on the Stac. A boy out of sight might be a boy missing, a boy fallen into the sea or wedged in a crevice, bones broken, or trapped on a ledge. The younger lads were content to sit crammed together in the Bothy, like puffins on a cliff. But the older ones had complicated things in their heads; things that needed to be thought through. Mr Farriss himself disappeared for hours at a time when the working day was done, and Quill was regularly sent to tell him supper was "now-or-never". Quill would find him sitting on some rocky terrace, staring out to sea in the direction of Hirta. As often as not, when told about the meal, he just shrugged, not minding whether he ate or not. Farriss simply wanted to be left alone.

Quill knew how he felt. He wanted it too: to be left alone to think about Murdina Galloway. If what Murdo said was true, then somehow Quill had brought her with him to the Stac. Everything he owned might be over yonder, lying in his home on Hirta, out of reach for ever. But he still had Murdina inside his head. And no one could take her from him.

So, when Quill was sent yet again to find Mr Farriss, he dawdled, and found himself a level place to sit that gave some relief to perpetually aching knees and hips. A few moments of privacy could not hurt; a half-hour watching the storm petrels eating their evening meal. The birds made spidery footprints on the waves, sipping invisible food out of the air.

Then he caught sight of the garefowl again – the same one bird who had roused up the gannet colony on the first day. She was standing on the landing place, the surging water winding her feet in lacy foam.

"It could swim away whenever it chose. Why does it stay?" asked a voice behind him.

Somehow Quill had passed right by Mr Farriss without seeing him. He was more scared than relieved at finding the man, who was lying on his side, curled up tight within a rocky cleft. The skin of his face seemed to have cleaved tight to his skull. He was nibbling the hairs from the backs of his fingers, and the hands were shaking. He did not even try to get up, but went on peering at the garefowl on the rocks below. "Why does it not step off? In the water it would be free of that great *body.*"

"This is not a bad place, Maister. If you're a bird. Like as not. Her kin live here. She calls the place home. Like as not."

But Mr Farriss was incapable of imagining contentment, even in a garefowl. "No. I have been watching it. It thinks to throw itself in the sea in despair. Like Fearnach Mor. But it lacks the courage."

Quilliam knew the story well enough, but he waited, out of politeness, for his teacher to tell it. "Mor was a sheep stealer, y'mind? He was caught and condemned to banishment in the worst place anyone could think of. This place. They put him in a boat and fetched him out here, and all the way he was cursing their eyes and their mothers. Vowing to change his ways. Swearing his innocence. Pleading for mercy – to be sent to a prison on the mainland – to be sent to Boreray – anywhere but the Warrior! So terrible was the prospect, that it took three men to get him out of the boat. And when they did, as the boat pulled away, Fearnach Mor threw himself into the sea and swam after it. Swam till he drowned."

To Quill, it seemed singularly unlikely that the giant bird standing there on the shore, staring at her big feet, was contemplating suicide by drowning: garefowl can swim like fish.

"She's maybe lost her mate, Maister," said Quill. "She's maybe waiting for…"

"Aye. Like us," said Farriss. "Waiting. For a thing that will not come."

Quill thought of sidling away, so the man could weep in private. But the garefowl suddenly began preening herself, cracking open her stubby wings; shaking herself so all her plumes stood out. She looked directly up at him with her bandit mask and that club of a beak. *Stay*, she seemed to say.

So Quill racked his brain for a cheerful word. "He musta had a terrible bad conscience, that Fearnach Mor. All those crimes he did. They musta weighed him down – the thought of all those sheep he thieved?" And he bent his knees, stumbled about and mimed the villain staggering under the burden of a dozen sheep weighing on his mind. (What made him do it? Who jokes when their teacher is lying out in the rain like an upturned crab waiting for the gulls to eat it?) "Maybe he didna jump at all! The ghosts of all those sheep came and toppled him into the sea! He lacked for goodwill, that's what... Ma says you can be happy anywhere, with a jar of goodwill and clean ears."

Mr Farriss smiled despite himself. "Is that what your ma says? Has she lived in many anywheres?"

"Just Hirta. But she's always cheery – and a marvel with the corner of a pinafore. Even our sheep have clean ears."

"And goodwill?"

"It's good wool with sheep. 'Good wool 'n' clean ears'."

Farriss sat up. They both watched the awkward flailing of a gigantic garefowl preening herself, and questioned how garefowl managed to keep their ears clean. Farriss was not convinced they had ears at all, so Quill whistled, to find out, and the bird looked round straight away. "They maybe help each other out with the preening and the ear-cleaning," he speculated, "and that's why they live all crammed up together."

Farriss looked at him, eyes not-quite-focused for want of sleep. He had bitten so hard into the corner of his bottom lip that it had swollen and bled. He had twisted tufts of hair out of his hairline, too, and left a row of little white holes. "I cannot help you boys, Quilliam."

"We can look out for ourselves, Maister."

Abruptly, Farriss stood up. "You have fortitude, Quilliam," he said, without looking at him. "When the men go down, the other boys will need you." And he walked back towards Midway Bothy, rock shale falling from his clothes like pieces of eggshell.

Quill did not follow. For some reason, he climbed down the scree slope towards the sea, for a closer look at the solitary garefowl. How likely was it to be the same bird as before? On the other side of the Stac, or over on Boreray, there might be hundreds of identical birds standing shoulder-to-shoulder.

Perhaps garefowl are so sleek and fat that the fear slides off them. Or else they are born stupid. The bird did not shy away. She simply muttered to herself – like the Owner's Steward when he visited Hirta to collect the rent: always making calculations under his breath and noting down numbers in his little ledger.

Quill said, "Hello. I'm King Gannet. Remember me?"

The soft mutterings went on, the bird rocking to and fro, balancing her great weight on one foot at a time.

"Has the world ended, d'you know?"

The garefowl opened wide her stubby, flightless wings and rattled them. Lit by the setting sun, the spray fanned out like golden seed. Her flat feet made patterns on the landing place, which the next wave wiped out. She mumbled to herself, hoarse and crabby. But after a time, the noise came to sound more like Gaelic with a thick, mainland accent. And, inside his head, Quill could see Murdina Galloway printing the sand with her bare, white feet. He could even hear her singing:

The water is wide, I cannot cross o'er
And neither have I wings to fly.

Something had happened on Hirta. End of the world or not, their people were *not* coming to fetch them off the Stac. They would have come if they could, but they could not. No one was coming. No one would ever come…unless it was God's angels and Judgement Day. Quill realized that, like Fearnach Mor, he had been pleading inwardly for some different outcome, all the time hoping for a reprieve. Now the truth fell on him, like an icy, breaking wave: no one was coming. They were marooned on Warrior Stac, no matter why. Ships go down at sea and all aboard them drown: it happens all the time. And on every one of those ships the sailors and passengers must have been hoping, up to the very last moment, for some twist of fate to save them.

Quill wanted to get the crying out of the way before he had to go back to the Bothy. But that music was still like a frenzy in his head, trying to stop him thinking:

Give me a boat that will carry two
And both shall row, my love and I.

So he shut his eyes and, instantly, he pictured himself walking up to the family rig – the strip of land where they grew wheat and vegetables. A girl was standing there on the fresh-hoed earth, sprinkling seeds. They fanned out from her hand like golden water drops.

Murdina?

Hello, Quilliam.

Will you come with me, Miss Galloway?

Maybe. I like travelling. Where were you meaning?

Some of us are going out to the stacs. Fowling for fulmar and guga. You can come if you care to? Stow away on the boat? Creep ashore and hide, and we can meet in secret and there'll be maybe a corner in the Bothy where no one ever looks, and you can hide there and no one will know.

I would like that, Quill. You have fortitude. And very curly hair. You are sure to become King Gannet, and a king's a fine match for any…

A damp weight pressed heavily against Quill's leg, and his eyes flew open in fright. The garefowl, lonely for her mate or the massed flock, was leaning against his shin, studying him with her bandit eyes. He reached out and stroked her back.

And the fright eased. That's to say…he laid it by. Like a dead bird, it would keep for later.

When he got back to the Bothy, there was no supper left for him. In place of it, "Minister" Cane served him up a little sermon about the sin of dawdling. Murdo was angry, too, because he had been worried by Quill's lateness: a boy late might be a boy fallen to his death. Mr Farriss cast anxious looks in his direction, as if he should never have confided so much in a mere boy.

But Quilliam did not need supper, or a lecture, or Mr Farriss's trust. He curled himself up in his sleeping place and shut out every sound but the singing in his head:

Oh never will I married be until the day I die,

Since the raging seas and stormy winds parted my love and I.

He looked inside his skull, like a cleit, and found it full to the brim with imaginings that might just sustain him through the bad times ahead. The weight of rock towering above him weighed less heavily. And despite his rumbling stomach, he slept.

6

Confessions

Every day someone else came face-to-face with the same thing. That moment, when fretting turned to knowing for certain: they were all alone. No one was coming. One evening, it even happened to John – round, jolly, easy-going John, who never seemed to do "fretting" at all. John went out of the mouth of the Bothy and began calling: *"Mam! Mammy! Where are you?"* The littler ones, picking up on the panic, joined him, and they shouted and shouted until Domhnall Don bellowed at them to cease their row, and the "Minister" started to sing a hymn.

Unnerved and ashamed, the older boys went and plucked the younger ones forcibly indoors and shook them and called them a shame to their fathers, but panic is infectious, and they too were as jittery as sheep when the dogs are loose. Euan lent his sweet piping voice to Cane's hymn, but it did nothing to quell the rising tide of fear in the cave. Mr Farriss turned his face to the wall and covered his ears with both hands.

When the hymn finally finished and Quill could make himself heard, he piped up with "Who's for a story?"

"Minister" Cane was put out. Kenneth's lip rucked into a sneer.

"From the Bible?" asked Euan cautiously.

But Davie just scuttled across the floor to sit directly in front of Quilliam. In due course others crawled over to join him.

"Do you know why this place is called Warrior Stac?" They looked back at Quill blankly. "Minister" Cane began to humph and harrumph, as if he knew, but it was too complicated to explain.

"Because it looked like a Warrior?" asked Niall lamely.

"It did once, man. Once, when the sea was dryer and there were lanes across it where the ground showed through, the Amazon Queen came driving her chariot, all the way from Ireland."

And he saw their stampeding thoughts swing away from the precipice and trot to a stillness, mesmerized by the familiar music of storytelling.

"The news came of a dragon – a great fire-breathing dragon far away in the Northlands, where the monsters are made of ice. And, well, she had to go and fight it, because you hav'ta when a thing like a dragon turns up. But the people on Hirta said, 'What about us? What say the fairies invade – or pirates! – or a wave comes, tall as the sky, or a wind fit to capsize us? What say whales come, big as the Isle of Lewis?' They were sore afraid, I can tell you (though they were generally very brave). Then the Amazon Queen told one hundred and more of her armed men to stand one on another's shoulders, and with a wave of her chariot whip, she turned them into just one warrior, and ordered him to stand in the sea and guard the people of Hirta from all danger while she was gone, no matter what. And he stood and he stood, and the Queen drove away in her golden chariot. And he stood and he stood, till the sea filled up and covered all the dry lanes. And he stood and he stood, and got so blown on by the wind that, year by year, it tore every rag of clothing off his back. Even though he was mortal cold in his bare skin, he went on standing and standing, with the waves breaking and the wind plucking out his hair, because he had the bravery of a hundred men in his chest. And all the birds that were too tired or too heavy with eggs or had no wings to fly – like the garefowl hasn't – all took shelter in his armpits and his belly button and up his nose and all over every bit of him – which was good, because it kept him a bit warmed. And right up to this very day he stands here, because the Queen told him to look after us."

When Quill opened his eyes, the first face he took in was Davie's, gazing at him. The next was Col Cane's, his veiny cheeks and nose dark with rage. *"So! D'we have a pagan among us?"*

"Just a story," Quill said.

The younger boys were all looking round at the roof and walls of the Bothy, as if to identify what particular crease of the Warrior's body was keeping them safe.

"There's no help for us but in the Lord!" blared Cane in his best "Minister" voice.

"I didna mean…"

"The boy meant no harm," said Mr Farriss out of a corner of the cave untouched by candlelight.

"Will I cook you an egg, Col?" asked Domhnall Don in an effort to change the subject.

But the self-appointed Minister was too full of outrage to appreciate a supper of coddled eggs. "I d'na wonder this lout defiled the Lord's altar!"

There was a gasp. After a moment's bewilderment, Murdo understood and started to explain about needing the birding net out of the cleit before it got turned into an altar. But his words petered out as he saw Euan solemnly nodding his head, confirming that the cleit-altar had indeed been desecrated by Quill and Murdo and all its flowers scattered to the four winds.

"In the name of God, I forbid anyone to speak to this pagan boy for a week," proclaimed Cane, *"lest his unclean words creep in at your ears!"*

The little circle of listeners drew back obediently from Quill, and crawled away. Even so, they went to their sleeping places the warmer for a story to wrap themselves in. The Stac was not just a lump of rock, but a giant guardian who had tucked them into his pocket for safekeeping.

And Mr Don and Mr Farriss made a point of wishing Quill goodnight.

When "Minister" Cane declared it a sin to work on the Sabbath, none of the boys objected. They were bone weary from climbing, endlessly climbing, and from want of a comfortable night's sleep. Every one of them had accumulated bruises, grazes and sprains on the cliffs. The fear, too, was exhausting: the fear and the not knowing.

But Mr Don was appalled by the suggestion of letting Sundays go to waste. The summer was sliding away as inexorably as an outgoing tide. With it would go the birds. Though the fowling party had plucked and wrung their way through a mountain of birds, as far as Don was concerned, there could never be enough. Like the miser saving for his old age, he could think of nothing but providing for the dark and unknowable days to come. And of keeping the boys busy.

Mr Farriss backed him up: "We have winter bellies to think of. Better to work than to sit chewing on our own cud."

"The only purpose of Living is to think upon the Lord," Cane intoned, and his voice actually rose and fell as if he was considering setting the words to music.

Farriss was unimpressed. "And who's to say when it's Sunday, will you tell me? I've a loose enough hold on the month, leave alone the days of the week."

"Then it is as well the Holy Spirit enlightens me," said Cane with breathtaking arrogance. "I know in my soul when the Sabbath day dawns, as any *good* Christian does."

Farriss was less annoyed by the implied insult than by the folly of Cane's idea. As was Domhnall Don. He was Hirta's master craftsman: his big, strong hands could as readily build a stone wall as carve driftwood into spoons or knit a jerkin from the wool of his sheep. "We should be out seeking timber," he growled, "not sitting here on our arses. God helps them who strive to help theirselves. If we can once build a raft and get us over to Boreray…"

In the village Parliament, Farriss's and Don's votes would have outweighed Col Cane's. But here on the Stac, Cane had formed an unbeatable alliance – with God and with Fear and with Weariness. In a sermon half sung and half bleated, he warned the boys that if they dared to break Holy Law and work on a Sunday, they would be left behind whenever the Good Lord chose to send his angels down to Warrior Stac.

"Fowlers we are and foul we be indeed in the eyes of God! Think on your sins and repent!" he boomed that night before bed. It was not a lullaby anyone wanted to hear before sleeping, but Cane delighted in the sound of his own voice echoing around the Bothy.

Quilliam was relieved to find that no one obeyed Cane's ban on speaking to him. The older ones could not quite manage the leap from "Cane-the-gravedigger" to "Minister-Cane-who-must-be-obeyed". The young ones could not remember to obey it: when they thought a thing, it was out of their mouths before they could help it.

"What do people do in Heaven, Quill?" asked Davie next day.

"As we do, I suppose, only without ropes." And Quill described the angels clambering about the peaked clouds, gathering fowl and tucking the heads under the golden cords they wore around their waists till they bulged with gugas and ospreys and white swans.

But overhead the clouds were bruised black, brown and purple with pent-up rain. The sea bucked and heaved. The wall of stones now piled up in the mouth of the Bothy to keep out the wind, grated against one another. A squall swept through next day, swiftly followed by another and another. The fire lit to alert the angels would have been doused, if it had not been allowed to burn out long since: fuel was too precious. At least they managed to keep a flame alive in the Midway Bothy: since Minister Cane liked to eat his food hot, he was generous with the use of his tinderbox at mealtimes. Draughts from outside wrapped their heads in steam from the cooking pot – the one Davie's mother had lent in return for four eggs and three birds.

"How will my ma eat hot herself, Quill?" Davie asked, ambushed by tears every time the cooking pot appeared.

"She'll be at a neighbour's fireside is my guess," Quill said.

"What, she's not in Heaven?" Davie was aghast.

"Well that's what I meant," Quill said hastily. "D'ye think there's no neighbours to be had in Heaven? Or cooking pots? It's one long Christmas feast up there." And Davie nodded earnestly.

Through some slit or loop in the rocks overhead came an eerie yowling, like pure sorrow. Autumn winds brought the noise every night after that.

The old ways are powerful. Beliefs lingered on Hirta that were a thousand years old. For St Kildans, the isles and stacs fluttered with the souls of the dead, caught, like sheep's wool, on the stone walls or sharp rocks or thorn bushes. Every time the wind shrieked, it gave voice to some ghost stranded on a cliff edge or under a waterfall or down a ravine until its sins had been purged away by the weather. That was the noise they heard when the draughts howled through Midway Bothy. But whose ghosts were they *here*, howling in their ears? Drowned sailors wrecked against the cliffs? Fowlers fallen from the rocks on some summer trip to the Stac and left behind, unburied, by their friends?

"'Tis the ghost of Fearnach Mor," Kenneth hissed into the nape of Lachlan's neck, "come to slit your throat in the night."

"Nah!" Lachlan retorted. "He'd see your hulking carcass an' take you for a great sheep an' steal you away an' eat you up."

But a frisson of fear went through several who had overheard the whisper. Unlike Lachlan, they were easily scared by talk of ghosts.

The howling inspired a different fear in John, whose whisper arrived with the icy touch of a nose in the crease of Quill's neck. "Are *we* ghosts, would you say? D'you think maybe we drowned on the crossing and it's just our souls that reached here?"

The face was too close to focus on, but Quill took in tears and an awful ashy pallor. Why did they keep asking *him* these unanswerable questions? Why should he know? He had cramp in his calves from five hours' cliff work and he was certainly not feeling like a disembodied soul. "Nah. We would recall. You dunna forget a thing like dying. Why would you say it?"

But the tears still trickled down. The two of them took John's problem outside. "Well, we mighta been put here till all our sins are blown off us – like the Warrior's clothes were blown off him! ...D'you reckon sin looks like blood, Quill?" John reached inside the waistband of baggy, inherited trousers. The fingers that emerged were bloody.

"Tell someone," was Quill's reaction.

"I am. I'm telling you." John seemed ashamed at leaking life blood. Quill was simply scared. What if it was a catching disease? Or a fate they might all start to suffer? He mustered possible explanations for a sudden up-welling of blood. When, last year, Mrs Campbell's boy had fallen to his death, blood had spilled from his mouth and ears: Quill had seen it. "Did you have a fall today?"

"Nowowo!" groaned John.

When fulmars puked up the contents of their stomachs, the liquor was ruby red. "Did you maybe spill a fulmar when you tucked it under your belt?"

"Nowowo!"

And, of course, according to Murdo's older sister, once a month grown women bled, to prove they were not pregnant...

John was rocking to and fro, clutching a griping belly ache. Bare feet emerged from the ragged ends of ancient trousers. The ankles were skinny, not like Quill's. Kilda men are bird-men – thick-ankled with toes that splay out as birds' do. It was pointless studying the big, round face: John's hair was chopped off short; the skin was chipped by rock shale and chapped by wind.

"John, can I ask you a thing? Is there a chance... Could you maybe..." But Quill stammered to a halt. If he was wrong, he would certainly get his nose broken: John had a powerful pair of fists. There is no acceptable way of asking a mate, a fellow, another boy... *Are you a girl, by any chance?*

"Women bleed that way once a month," he suggested tentatively. "Or so Murdo says. 'S natural. They dunna come to harm from it, far as I know." He watched what effect his words had on John.

"They do?"

"That's what Murdo says. And he has sisters."

"Did he say it gives them belly ache?"

"He said it makes them ratty."

Head bowed, eyes closed, John seemed about to make Confession. And she did.

Apparently, John's mother had given birth to eight children, but seven had died. (This much Quill vaguely knew. It was not an unusual story: not on Hirta.) But when the eighth was born a girl, the mother thought her husband might just die of disappointment: he was that set on having a son. So, she cut the cord herself, wrapped the baby tight and told her husband it was a boy. The "boy" had been named John and raised accordingly. The truth was kept even from John. After all, who would be hurt by one well-meaning little lie?

No one, perhaps, but John.

"I couldna grasp it: why I kept spraining ma ankles. An' ma voice was pitched so high. An' in them pissing contests – why could I never win ever? Not once? I thought I was born wrong – a useless piece o' sheepshite – an' I sank into a gloom. In the end, Ma hadta say. Told me, on condition I never *ever* told Father nor any other soul. Said she'd die of shame if I did. *So you mustn't tell!*" John concluded in a panic.

"Who would I tell?" said Quilliam. "Did she say anything about blood, your ma?"

John shook her head. "She shoulda! She shoulda told me! It's no fair."

Quill could not help agreeing: it was not fair to have left John in ignorance. Perhaps the poor woman liked to pretend to herself that John truly was a boy. Or maybe she had plain forgotten. But the more Quill thought about it, the more unkind it seemed – to cut John off from all those girl things she might have liked or wanted: the red headscarves, the blue dresses, the penny brooch every woman wore, the singing at the work-tables – marriage even! – and a baby's crib at the foot of the bed…

But of course John was right: Quill must not tell her secret – not here, not now. The girls went fowling together. The boys went fowling together. But mix the two and it would be like putting candles into a sack of feathers. "Best keep it 'twixt you and me," said Quilliam. "Could make all manner of trouble."

She nodded dumbly. Then asked what he meant.

His own mother had always said: *Kindness doesna cost a penny, Quill.* He must find something kind to say now. "Well, think of the duels, man! The broken hearts! All the boys would be after marrying you! You being so…bonny, n'all."

John coloured with pleasure. "Had you guessed already, then?"

"Nooo! Well…I had an inkling, maybe – you being so…wee and fragile."

John was so grateful that she pumped his hand fiercely for fully a minute, and wept like a – well – like a girl.

Quilliam was so grateful to Murdo for having told him about the monthly-mysteries-of-women, that he naturally went straight to find his friend and told him that John was, in fact, a girl. "You're to tell no one, ever, y'hear? No one. I promised."

"Who would I tell?" Murdo said and shrugged. But a peculiar look came over him that Quill could only interpret as a flicker of hope.

"Minister" Cane decided next that everyone must confess their sins to him once a week. Somehow, without it ever being discussed, Cane had retired from fowling to become a full-time priest.

The idea must have come to him suddenly, and pleased him so much that he did not even wait for evening prayers to announce it, but sent Euan to seek out every boy and tell them the time of day and day of the week to report, in pairs, for their appointed Confession. Just maybe it was also Cane's way of bypassing Mr Don and Mr Farriss. Had he announced his plan to everyone at supper, the men's laughter or roars of protest might have damaged the "Minister's" air of holiness. Cane firmly believed in his air of holiness. He had taken to holding the front of his jacket as he had seen Reverend Buchan hold the lapels of his coat. If he was going to be a minister of the kirk, he definitely needed both hands free to hold his lapels and look grand. Hence the need to give up fowling.

Domhnall Don quite swelled up with rage when he finally heard about the summons to Confession. His jowls turned purple, and he threw down the bird he was plucking. "By the soul, are we Catholics now? Only foreigners and Catholics 'confess their sins'. What, is he the Pope? And will someone tell me: does he have the power to forgive sins now?" Mr Farriss, too, filled up with disgust, the small blood vessels showing blue in his temples – but he said nothing. Like an oyster, that swallows sharp grit then shuts its lips tight, Farriss rarely put his feelings into words. Anyway, he and Don had rather surrendered responsibility for the boys' souls to Col Cane (simply because neither of them felt equal to it). So perhaps they were partly to blame for the man puffing himself up. Still, if Cane thought Don and Farriss were going to "confess their sins" to him, he could think again.

The cave that evening was full of boys trying to think of something to confess. When their eyes turned to Quill for a suggestion, he put up his two hands defensively. "Dunna ask me. How should I know?"

He seemed to have been given some fearful new role to play: "the one blessed with Good Ideas" – and he could not quite think why. Was this what it was to be King Gannet? No, that was just about being good at climbing. Quill could not remember being anything but run-of-the-mill ordinary, back on Hirta. And yet...and yet, looking back to his boyhood, he could remember older boys seeming different – more trustworthy – more something... Could it be that a boy reached an age when he had to start being someone different – someone people could apply to for help, for answers? The thought petrified him.

But when John crept over and asked him, "Quill, must I tell the Minister about me being...you know...?" he shook his head so emphatically that Kenneth, even through the smoke of the cooking fire, scented a secret and roused himself like a dog scenting meat.

Kenneth, of course, had plenty of sins he could confess to – ought to confess to. By rights, Kenneth ought to say sorry for being born, but it is a strange kind of bully who lies awake nights fretting about his crimes. So it was startling when he got up during the evening meal, in front of everyone, and said to Col Cane, cold as sea-glass, "What we should do is tell you what *other* boys have done bad." The mischief was shining so bright in Kenneth's eye: Cane could surely read the villainy in him.

But "Yes!" said the "Minister", unable to keep the eagerness out of his voice. "Yes! That shall be the way of it, Kenneth. Good lad. Each boy may either confess his own faults, or tell me the sins of another boy. Then all shall be known."

Was Kenneth mad? Surely everyone would use their Confession to tell how Kenneth had sworn at them, how Kenneth had punched them, how Kenneth had tripped them or twisted their arm or smashed the eggs they were carrying... Though no. A moment's thought said that that would never happen. Of course it wouldn't. No one tells tales on a bully, for fear the bully makes him pay afterwards.

Kenneth looked around the cave with a smug leer. His eye rested a while on every boy in turn, and the look on his face asked: *What shall I tell him about* you?

"You'll not tell about John's...secret, will you?" Quill whispered to Murdo. He knew the idea was in Murdo's head because, just for an instant, he had wondered about telling it himself.

"Why would I? It's no a sin to be a girl." And Murdo managed to be outraged at the suggestion (for all he had given it a thought). "We shouldna tell the man spit. No business of his what anyone's done." And his hands made fists and punched the air. Lately, there was a frenzy in Murdo that scared Quill. It is an awful thing when a friend alters from how you like them to be. Quill laid a calming hand on him, but Murdo threw it off as if Quill might steal some of the anger out of him, when he needed it all for himself.

"Tell you what: let's say what we *havena* done," Quill suggested. "Not prayed enough. Not worked hard enough. Forgot our sums. Despairing's a sin. We could confess to Despair."

"I havena *despaired*," Murdo snapped.

"I know it. I was only saying..."

And Murdo did agree it was the best way to go: to confess to their "did nots" instead of their "dids". So, attending Confession at the duly appointed time, kneeling in front of the so-called "Minister", they owned up to sins of omission:

"I didna pray before I slept last night."

"I've forgot the Ten Commandments."

"I didna spread the ash on the floor when Mam asked it."

"I fell asleep in the kirk while the Reverend Buchan was speaking."

"I think I despaired last Thursday. Just for a minute. Mighta been Friday."

"And what can you tell me of the sins of others?"

"Nothing, Mr Cane."

"*Minister* Cane," said the village gravedigger.

But Quill had made John a promise. He had also made himself a promise – that he would never address Col Cane as "Minister". "Nothing, Mr Cane," he repeated, and Cane fetched him a blow with the back of his hand.

Quilliam told no one about Mr Cane hitting him, but someone must have done, because suddenly the boys were terrified. Like Murdo and Quill, they had joked about what they would confess to, or who they would accuse, and say, *He picked his teeth. He snored in my ear.* Now, they were threatened with violence. There was no more laughter.

St Kildans are gentle people – Quill knew that because Murdina had said as much: *Such lovely, gentle people, you are: happy as robins perched on your little island kingdom,* she had said.

"*If Cane hits me, I'll kill him!*" Lachlan burst out.

The others stared at him, his face puce with rage, his teeth bared like a dog. "*Not here. Not here. Not here, he willna! Not nobody willna! Not here!*" And he glared around at the other boys, as if he had thought of the Stac as his safe haven only to find it threatened by a man with fists.

7

Miracles

Days of the week seemed important, and not just for the sake of knowing when Sunday came round yet again or the right day for Confession. How was a Thursday different from a Tuesday? The boys ate the same, did the same work, thought the same thoughts. And yet they were forever asking: "What day is it, Quill?" "Is it Friday, Quill?" "Is it Monday?" The days of the week are like when you are going down a cliff, feeling about with one foot and needing to find the next foothold. If they're not there when you feel for them, it can be unnerving.

But why did they have to keep asking *him*? Irritability had beset them like an outbreak of ringworm, and Quill was as riddled with it as everyone else. His nose ran incessantly, making his top lip hideously sore. And yet the noise of Calum sniffing, or yet another person asking, *What day is it, Quill?* was far worse: they dripped on to his nerve-endings like scalding water. Quill breathed deeply, found himself a sharp stone and began scratching a calendar above his sleeping place. Randomly, he decided it was October.

Domhnall Don had scratched a picture, too, of the raft he was building. How do you build a raft on a spike of rock where nothing grows bigger than lichen and limpets? You let the sea bring the makings to you. The sea delivers up all manner of things: flotsam. Splinters of disaster. You don't have to hold the thought of them too hard or the splinter makes your heart bleed, but sometimes, far out at sea somewhere, a wave smashes into a ship, washes baskets and barrels and crates overboard, and sometimes even the mast.

Sometimes the crew.

All sorts of boats turn tail and run from storms towards St Kilda, meaning to beach themselves in Hirta's Village Bay or shelter in the lee of the stacs. But some get caught in a rip tide, dashed against cliffs and broken up like oatcakes. Or they wedge on the rocks and the sea pulls them apart, plank by keel by deck by man...

Anyway. Pieces of timber turn up all the time. A plank might have been washing around the oceans of the world for years before it comes ashore, and the next storm might carry it away again. But Kildans gather it as they gather everything else – seaweed, shellfish, birds' eggs...

That was how Domhnall Don came to be building a raft. He had the boys on the watch for anything down by the water's edge, then came himself and dragged it ashore: a chunk of timber, a bit of barrel, a piece of keel, a wicker lobster pot. Things were piled now in Lower Bothy that no one could identify, knowing only that they had floated and might float again. Mr Don had Quill wriggling old nails out of timber, hoping to re-use them, to fasten everything together into a raft when the time came… He meant to cross over to Boreray. It was his way of doing something other than wait.

One day during her visit to Hirta, Murdina Galloway said she had taught the boys quite enough for one day and it was time for them to teach *her* something. So they taught her how to make egg baskets out of straw – for when they climbed up to cliff ledges to gather eggs and had no hands free to carry them back down.

"Your hands are always busy," said Murdina. "I've noticed that. If you are not knotting nets, you are weaving, or plaiting horsehair, or mending ropes, or plucking birds. I like that. I mean to be busy every moment I'm alive, and not waste one second…except when I'm sleeping, of course," she added, and laughed. And for some reason, it went through Quilliam's head that if there was one thing he wanted to see before he died, it was Murdina

Galloway's sleeping face in the dip of a pillow filled with feathers he had gathered himself.

They were sitting in The Street that day, mending ropes, and had their bare feet out enjoying the sunshine. Murdina looked at them and said, "God was so clever when he made you! He gave you the feet of birds and the ingenuity to outwit misfortune."

Quill had never heard the word before – "ingenuity" – but he could see perfectly well what it meant, and he kept it by him. In fact he pocketed lots of her words. It was like with the nails that came ashore in the bits of wooden flotsam. First he worked on them till he got them straight, then he pocketed them in case they came in handy… He could not have explained why he collected words, exactly. Nails were a lot more useful than words to the quiet-spoken people of St Kilda.

And when it came to Domhnall Don's raft, words would not get it built. It was going to take a lot of ingenuity, flotsam and nails for it to hold together as far as Boreray Stac, for all the place was so tantalizingly close. It was the search for flotsam that took a crowd of boys down to the waterline one day.

At least that was what they said they had been doing, when they told the men afterwards.

It is always dangerous to go down to the foot of the Stac. Even on the calmest days, the sea swells roll in.

Every seventh wave is bigger than the others, but you don't count the waves in case you count to nine by mistake and catch The Kilda Gloom and it fills up your head with black thoughts. So it is easy to be caught off-guard by wave number seven.

Kenneth (who said he did not believe that the world had ended) had been teasing Euan for days, calling him "Our Little Angel" and "God's doggie"; saying Euan "only wants to be an angel so he can wear a dress". Teasing. Such a woolly little word for what Kenneth did once he decided to persecute another boy for the fun of it.

Euan, gentle as a lamb, had a core of iron in him, though. However much Kenneth made fun of his "holy vision", his belief in angels, his gathering of flowers for the cleit-altar, and his hymn singing, Euan kept doggedly on, praying for Kenneth and everybody else, too.

Finding the Little Angel lying prostrate in front of the altar one day, arms outstretched, face pressed out of shape by the chilly rock, Kenneth stood on Euan's back and said, "Can you walk on water? Walk on water, can you? Can you? Got enough faith and y'can walk on water. Read it in the Bible, I did."

That Kenneth had ever read anything was unlikely, but he was not wrong about the story. Anything concerning the sea interested the people of St Kilda, so the story of Jesus walking on the Sea of Galilee was a particular favourite at the kirk. "*So his good friend Peter climbs out of the boat, and starts to walk over the waves...until it suddenly goes through his head that the thing can't be done, and his faith fails him and he starts to sink. Jesus has to reach out a hand to stop Peter drowning.*" The congregation would nod, easily able to picture it. They had seen countless storm-petrels skip over the water without their feet ever sinking in.

Now here was Kenneth, telling Euan, "You should do it. Everyone knows you're the saint round here." And before he had stepped off Euan's ribcage, he had made Euan promise to try walking over the sea, to Boreray Stac.

Kenneth picked his time, carefully. Next day, he waited until everyone else was working the cliffs, feigned a pulled muscle and said he could not work. Then he mustered an audience – just to add to Euan's humiliation when the boy lost his nerve. It was not an audience of men, of course, or older boys, but the little ones, the little gullible ones who thought they were about to see a "miracle": Lachlan, Niall, Davie.

Quill and John were sharing a rope. Their rope was tied off round a spire of rock. It was John who spotted the cluster of boys down by the landing place, Kenneth looming large alongside skinny littler ones. She pointed them out to Quill, who sniffed the air. The smell of mischief reached him on the up-draught.

But climbing up a rope, laden with birds, is a slow process, particularly when there is no rope-man at the top to pull you up.

"What's the drop below you?" Quill called down, and John estimated it was safer to climb down rather than up. They had to drop painfully onto a ledge below, and sidle their way down and round in the direction of the huddle of boys. They were close enough to see the grin on Kenneth's face, but not close enough to be heard if they shouted into the wind.

The bully was in fact declaiming, in mock, shocked tones, "Never *knew* you were *such a mouse*, Euan! Can't *believe* you're such a *worm*, such a *girl*, such a Doubting Thomas. Such an *unbeliever.*" The other boys were tittering, but uneasy, too, and disappointed. A miracle would have been exciting.

Unaware of the dare, Quilliam climbed cautiously down towards the cove. The cliff was steep, and it would be foolish to risk a fall by hurrying. So he was still high up, and got a good aerial view of the moment Euan gave in to Kenneth's bullying.

Euan simply walked across the shelf of rock creamy with foam, and kept on walking, out on to open water.

The sea ate him up.

Kenneth's jaw dropped. He stretched out a hand as if to grab the moment back out of mid-air. He made another futile grab with the other hand as Lachlan came pelting past and threw himself into the sea.

"*Never thought he'd do it!*" Kenneth was yelping for the seventh time as John and Quill came sliding down the rock face. "*I never thought…!*"

The seventh wave rose up, huge, and they all saw Euan hanging, outstretched, in its transparency. Then he was gone again, and the cold of the big wave broke over their thighs and sent the little ones reeling. It was devastating, that cold. The muscles of their legs went rigid, also their brains. They simply stared at the hollow dip behind the wave: a shining bowl holding nothing, nothing.

Then Lachlan surfaced, alone. He looked to right and left, saw nothing, upended himself and disappeared again, his kicking feet leaving a flummery of foam on the surface. When he came up next, he had Euan by the scruff of his jacket.

Lachlan trod water, looking landwards, just like the seals off the village beach. He made no effort to swim towards them. Euan blinked and began to struggle, but Lachlan only held him by the face and told him sharply, "Be still." He was counting the waves. When, looking over his shoulder, he saw a large swell rise up like the back of a whale, he let it carry him and Euan hurtling towards the Stac. Any cross-current and the wave would smack them both dead against the rock face.

But the shelf caught them like a shovel, and the wave slid out from under them and left a wet starfish of arms and legs jerking with cold.

Euan was at last brought to tears – not by Kenneth, not by fright or cold, even. But by his failure to walk on water.

Kenneth was appalled. *"What was he thinking? Idiot! Ninny! Numbskull! Got cheese for brains, or what?"* He had never imagined for a moment that the Little Angel would take up the dare – would believe for one moment that it could be done – would dare to be so stupid. *"Just teasing, I was! Just joking!"*

Just trying to make the child cry and grovel.

And then *Lachlan* had gone in too! Poor Kenneth: bewilderment sat on him like a wet sheep and squeezed all the breath out of him.

As for Lachlan, if boys had tails, his would have been wagging. He was a hero. Quilliam would have given him a gold sovereign (if he had ever had one). With the exception of Kenneth, they could none of them wait to get back to the Bothy and tell what Lachlan had done.

"But you canna," said John. She jerked her head in the direction of Euan, gibbering and shivering and wretched. "Poor wee man. Does he no feel bad enough without you telling the men and the big boys he tried to do a miracle?"

It was true. They could not tell what had happened without adding to Euan's misery and humiliation – also without fetching down adult rage on everyone involved.

So when they got back to the cave, they said that Euan had fallen in trying to pull some driftwood ashore for Mr Don's raft, and Lachlan had jumped in and saved him.

The surge of exclamations and whistles and murmurs of admiration drew eyes away from Euan and left him no need to say anything at all.

They stripped both swimmers, and rubbed them warm with their woollen hats. An assortment of ragged clothing was temporarily loaned them by the other lads.

"Minister" Cane stood up. "Let us give thanks to God," he said in his gloomy, booming voice, as if he resented all the attention going to rag-a-boy Lachlan.

Quilliam was still silly with relief. "Yes, but let's give thanks to Lachlan, too!" he told the room at large. "I say *he* should be King Gannet now!" The room whooped in agreement. Cane glowered.

There were usually furrows in Lachlan's forehead, like a permanent frown, even when he smiled; it made him look like a little old man. Now his whole face shone, he gave a gurgling giggle and did a little dance (which was not simply to get warm). "By all the fishes in the sea, I *love* this place!" he said.

It took a moment for Quill to realize that Lachlan meant the Stac. He meant Warrior Stac – this jet-black spike of dumb rock where they were trapped, like as not until the day they died; away from their people, away from their dogs, away from beds and porridge and rigs and everything joyful. And yet Lachlan of the permanent frown was as happy as anyone had ever seen him.

8

Outcast

The gannets were leaving. It was the gannets which had brought them to the Stac. Now, every day, more gannet families rose from the cliffs, like flakes of white paint peeling off a wall, and were blown out to sea. They did not return. Their winters were spent at sea. Unlike the fowlers, they could leave at will. The cliffs were blacker – bleaker – without them. The sight of them flying out to sea added to the feeling of being completely abandoned.

Suddenly, every day was the Sabbath.

The "Minister" said that everyone must stop fowling and give over each waking hour to prayer and hymn-singing and wringing their souls to see what dirty water dripped out. He personally undertook to lead them to salvation.

Domhnall Don gave one of his rare, honking laughs and shook his head in disbelief. Mr Farriss groaned and turned his face to the wall. The boys, of course, greeted it as a kindness – not to have to leave the cave. The weather was no longer friendly. Outside the Bothy a cold wind was invariably lying in wait for them. Rain-sodden clothes did not dry so readily without a warm sun to dry them.

They had begun to look like survivors of war or shipwreck, haggard and hollow-eyed. They would sit picking at the scabs on their knees, comparing bruises, rubbing bird oil into open cuts and grazes in the hope of keeping them from going bad.

Is no one going to argue? thought Quill. It was insane. The birds would be gone soon. The party must keep fowling for as long as possible. There were cleits needed mending. There was Mr Don's raft to build. He was right! Don was right! With a raft they could get to Boreray! There were a couple of derelict shepherds' shelters there – and sheep! – and peat they could cut and burn to keep warm. It might be as empty of life as Warrior Stac, but its rounder contours promised ease and comfort in comparison with this bestial horn of a rock.

The chief reason Quill recoiled from the thought of workless days stuffed with worship was the prospect of idleness. He leaned over and whispered to Murdo, "We need to keep *busy*, man. 'S important to stay busy, right?" They needed to pass the time, so that Time did pass. Otherwise…otherwise they would all slide to a stop and sit and be helpless, which is next to being dead.

People are better for being busy. Murdina Galloway had said so.

Quill stood up. "We ought to keep on *doing*."

Everyone turned to stare at him. Even Mr Farriss uncurled himself. Quill thrust his hands deep into his pockets, as if his hands had done the talking and were taking shelter. When nobody spoke, he felt obliged to plough on. "Why did God give us bird feet and make us ingenious if He wanted us just to sit about and do nothing? This is a test, maybe! Of our ingenui…tousness." He paused again, soaked up the silence, and felt damper for it. "Anyway, we should keep busy. That's what I think. The Devil makes work for idle hands, Ma says."

Col Cane was so shocked at being contradicted that he could find nothing to say, and settled for looking sickened: he had a face made for it. At last he choked out: "Lo! The boy Quilliam has spoken! In his BIG WORDS."

And Quill realized: Cane had no idea what "ingenious" meant – which was gratifying. It was the first time Quill had known something that a grown man did not: "ingenuity". At the selfsame moment his fingers, nervously gripping a useless bent nail in his pocket, suggested the thing was not useless after all, and might make a good fish hook if they ran short of bird meat. An ingenious thought.

Not that Quill's opinion made the smallest difference. Nor did the opinions of Domhnall Don or Mr Farriss, who agreed with Quill and continued to go out on to the Stac every day, Don looking for flotsam, Farris trying to escape his worries, like a dog trying to flee his own fleas.

"Well? Who's coming to do his work?" growled Mr Don as he left the cave carrying rope and saddle. But the boys hung back. Col Cane had told them that every day was now the Sabbath on Warrior Stac, and if they worked on the Sabbath, it would be "on pain of eternal damnation". The words were fearful enough to hold them in thrall to a pompous, ignorant man they neither liked nor respected. Quilliam made to stand up, but Murdo pulled him down again – maybe to save Quill from damnation but, more probably, to stop Quill betraying friends who preferred not to work.

"We need to keep busy," hissed Quill. "We need the birds! You wanta starve, man?"

Kenneth overheard. "Ach, if we run outa food, I'll turn to eating the small ones." And he pointed his lop jaw at Davie, licked his lips and laughed.

For a time, the "Minister" heard their "Confessions", two by two, in front of the altar-cleit outside. When it got too cold for his liking, he turned everyone out of the cave and had them stand about in the raw wind, until he had finished interrogating each boy in turn. Working keeps you warm, but standing about is wicked chilling.

Even when Don and Farriss came back from fowling, they soon enough went out again – no longer to share a pipe of tobacco, since their tobacco was all gone, but to be somewhere free of boys and somewhere they could avoid the sight of Cane.

So neither man was there that evening when Col Cane unmasked the demon among them.

"I hear we have one among us who *does not believe*," he announced, while dinner bubbled in the pot, begging to be eaten.

Euan raised his head off his knees, panic-stricken, but he was not the guilty party. It was not Euan's failure to walk on water that had appalled Col Cane.

"There is one here who *does not believe the world has ended*! One who has fallen into the *black pit of wickedness* and is full of lewd thoughts. One whose black soul is caked in *witchery*."

That grabbed everyone's attention. Even Quilliam was riveted to know which of them had confessed to "witchery".

It never entered his head that it might be him.

"Davie tells me he has seen this boy 'talking with a sea-witch down by the water'," brayed Col Cane.

Davie's mouth dropped open. He looked from Quill to the "Minister" and back again. "I only said… It was a fine thing! I only said, Quill – cross my heart and hope to die! I said it was a fine thing, the way the bird huddled up close!"

"A *fine thing*, is it, child, to commune with *phantoms and demons*?" Cane intoned. Davie spluttered and stammered, trying to put right the misunderstanding, but the "Minister" was wielding his power, as a smith wields a hammer. He pointed at Quill. "There is more. Stand up, loutish boy. Not only have you consorted with the sea-witch, but Kenneth informs me that you have 'done sins of the flesh' with the niece of Mr Farriss."

"That's a lie!"

Some there gasped (chiefly at the fact that Cane was ready to repeat secrets told him in confidence). Kenneth sniggered.

"And now you incite the lads to defy my commandments and work on the Sabbath!"

Within the minute, Quill had been repainted as the very portrait of sin, disobedience and witchery.

Quill thought everyone would laugh – that someone – anyone – would laugh. But nobody did. They just stared at him: fearful, incredulous.

Then Kenneth picked up a sliver of shale and threw it at Quill. Murdo rose from his place in anger, but the "Minister" laid a blessing on Kenneth's head, stroking his hair. "Yes, laddie. We canna let the witch foul our nest, nor sully our minds." And picking up a pebble, Cane threw it – less accurately than Kenneth, but plainly inviting every boy there to let fly. Half-heartedly, uncertainly, the boys looked around them for pebbles. "That's right, laddies. The

Lord instructs us to cast out demons in His name. Let us cast this demon Quilliam into the Outer Darkness."

There are times for arguing, explaining, protesting: this was not one. Quill was out of there without even stooping to pick up his hat.

No one with a morsel of sense moves about the cliffs at night. But Quill did. He slid and scrambled downwards, hoping to meet with Farriss or Don and plead for help. But they were nowhere in sight. The sky was seeded with birds – some furtive, fearful breed that only flew home after sunset. They sped inshore so fast that they seemed to hurl themselves into extinction against solid rock. Three or four times, one passed so close by that Quill thought it had collided with him, the thrum of wings was so loud against his ear.

Just as furtive and fearful, Quill made for a burrow of his own – made for Lower Bothy, to be out of sight of the moon, though all he could make out of Night's geography was the jagged metal floor of the sea far below. Everything else was a black mass of nothingness. He could not even see the rock face he was climbing down – what jags and snags were inflicting so many grazes, bruises and cuts.

It was madness to think he could find Lower Bothy in the dark. Within minutes he was lost. Within the hour, he had so over-strained his arm muscles that his hands were jumping like frogs; he lay flat along a ledge, feeling them twitch and cramp and scrape against dried spikes of bird lime, and could not think they were his hands at all. Nothing was in his control, not his hands, not anything. Somehow he had become Quill the Witch, possessed by demons. In fact he could feel the demons inside him, like burning turf in his guts: Rage, Loathing, the longing to clap Col Cane inside his own church bell and hit it with a peat spade over and over and over until Cane's teeth fell from his mouth, the tartan from his plaid and the smugness from his miserable, sagging jowls...

Quill wished he had not left behind his woollen cap: there was nowhere smooth to lay his face. He started to wonder what else he had left behind, and the last and worst fear that came was that he had left Murdina.

In the Bothy, she had come to his sleeping place at his bidding, but if she came tonight, Quill would not be there. And she was not a witch, not a witch, not a witch, not any kind of witch! There are men who can make a rabbit out of a knotted handkerchief, to make their babbies laugh. Quill could make Murdina out of memories and imagination and the softness of a rolled-up jacket. But now he was banished and hated and alone. Perhaps even Murdina would shun him, persuaded by Col Cane's sanctimonious lies. At least God was out of earshot here on the Stac. God would not be taken in by the man's drivelling malice.

Quill knew now how Fearnach Mor, the sheep-stealer, had felt, condemned to marooning; carried out by boat to live till he died, alone on the Stac. Now Quill knew what had made the thief hurl himself into the sea and swim after the boat, pleading for mercy.

The moon was setting. Its wake of moonshine dwindled towards the horizon. Soon Quill would be plunged into utter blackness. And he, too, wanted to yell at the moon: *Wait! Don't go! I'll change! I'll mend my ways! I've done nothing!* Next he knew, he was drowning in dark.

At first light, he woke, stiff as a plank of flotsam, his ribcage so rigid with cold that he could barely breathe. In the dark he had strayed a mile round the Stac. Finding the Lower Bothy cost him hours of climbing. More than once, blackbacks came after him, beaks like filleting knives. The wind shifted, and rain gathered on the horizon, like stooks of mildewed rye.

"*I've done nothing! I did nothing!*" he shouted at the beleaguering storm clouds. There came no reply but for the first drops of rain, falling on him like spittle.

Even the sea was hostile to witchy Quilliam: the waves hissed. The temperature plummeted. The rain doused the embers of anger scorching Quill's guts, but he was not grateful: Rage was all that had been keeping him going.

By the time he found Lower Bothy, his flesh was jumping with cold. Dead red jellyfish lay rotting in a row across the doorway: his particular horror come to greet him. Theirs was the only colour anywhere, in any direction, as far as the edge of the world.

Hour after hour he watched the downpour hammering the sea flat. Noon was dark. Midnight was Stygian.

Next morning he passed the time piling up rocks across the cave's entrance, to keep out the wind. Without fire, he knew full well he would die quite soon. The fulmars were flying out to sea. The gannets had gone. Kilda's larder was dwindling. The Warrior would soon have no crumbs left in his pocket to feed the children of Hirta. But, for now, there was a half-full cleit within reach from which he fetched back half a dozen birds. He thought fright and anger must have shrunk his stomach, but hunger crept into him again, under cover of hard work. He ate his first dried puffin as though it was Cane's right arm and he was tearing the flesh off it with his teeth. He ate the second, and savoured every bite.

Somewhere within the rock, the shearwaters began their unearthly chatter. It made for an eerie music. "*Like fairies spinning gold underground,*" Murdina had said when she first heard it. He repeated the words out loud – "Fairies spinning gold underground!" – and found he could breathe again. The cave was so cold that his breath made white mist as it came out of his mouth.

He was thirsty, and sucked at his wet clothes for the sake of the rainwater in them, wondering how he would catch enough to drink without any kind of pot to collect it in. Would he have to leave some piece of clothing out to soak up rainwater, then suck it dry? No, he could not spare a single item of clothing. If he was ever warm again (he told himself) it would be with lung fever or a direct lightning strike between the shoulder blades.

There were hollows and indentations in the terrace of rock outside, but he dared not drink from them in case the sea and not the rain had filled them. Salt water would only increase his thirst. Salt water could pickle his brains and turn him into a mad thing. In thinking it, a kind of hysteria trickled like salt water over his brain pan and made his vision blur, his head spin. He feared he was mad already.

With a flat-splatting noise, and bulk enough to block out a lot of daylight, something moved across the mouth of the cave. Quill scrabbled backwards, deeper into the cave, the heels of his hands leaning down on grit and sea slugs. What was it? A merman slapping his scaly tail on the smooth rocks? The blue-green men made of blue-green seawater, slopping sweat-salty onto the landing place and solidifying into flesh? His head banged the low rock roof at the back of the cave.

He was so scared that his eyes were slow to focus on the garefowl as she waddled by. She stopped – looked in – waddled on. A startling sight – but not fearful – that child-sized penguin, hunched and bulky-black. She roused

Quill out of his trance. He felt less alone and less afraid for seeing her.

Lower Bothy seemed huge without the men, the other boys, the piles of sacks and nets and ropes and egg baskets that had filled it on their arrival on Warrior Stac. He could have his choice of sleeping places. And yet nowhere seemed either dry or inviting, and the light was so much less than back in those summer days. Also, there was an unspeakable, sickening stench. Either he could live with it or he could hunt down the source and be rid of it.

The smell seemed to emanate from the darkest, lowest corner of the cave – a fissure too low to crawl under. So he lay on his stomach and groped at the darkness until his hands encountered...flesh.

The flesh disintegrated and oozed through his fingers, and left him holding bone. When he drew it out, the bone had teeth attached to it. Quill's stomach turned itself inside out so quickly and so violently that he was left sprawled in the mouth of the cave fighting for breath. He beat his stinking hand in the puddles of water – salt or fresh, he could never drink from them now – until he could rid himself of the smell.

There was fur, too: coarse, short hair.

He would go back up to Midway. He would tell them that some merman, some drowned sailor – Fearnach Mor, maybe – had died in the cave, and they would be so – what? – intrigued? sympathetic? – that they would let him stay. Or he would find some other cave to shelter in. But he had just raised himself to his hands and knees, shuddering and whimpering, when he saw three people watching him from the water.

So he was mad, after all. Desperation and cold had stolen his wits, and he had tumbled from Midway Bothy into a nightmare of horror and delusion.

"*Arff,*" said one of the three. "*Arff, arff.*"

Seals.

The noise that came out of Quill (though it was quite seal-like) scared the creatures away. They submerged and disappeared. Their sire, their grandsire, perhaps, had dragged himself into Lower Bothy to die. Or perhaps it had been washed ashore by a heavy swell, already dead, and become wedged in the very gullet of the cave. Quill laughed out loud that he could have thought anything else. The relief kept him going all the while he was excavating the rotting carcass from the back of the Bothy and returning it to the ocean. He kept as many of the bones as possible, in case they came in useful. "*Keep a thing seven year,*" his mother had said, "*and you shall find a use for it.*" Such a Kildan philosophy.

Quill prized the seal's skull most of all, because if he lay it on its back, on a high-up ledge outside the cave, it caught rainwater that he could safely drink.

As he lay down to sleep that night, he realized that he had no notion what day of the week it was, nor any way of finding out.

"Well, let it be Thursday," he said out loud.

And lo, it was Thursday! Who was to say otherwise? The boy who lives all by himself in the world is king of all he surveys. The thought made him smile.

Next day, Murdo came.

"They sent me to see if you were here."

"Who did?"

"Mr Farriss and Domhnall Don. They had us searching yesterday, but the rain came on too hard and we had to stop, case'n we fell in the dark. I knew ye'd be here. Have your bonnet." And he thrust Quill's woollen hat at him, along with his own knife and two sacks: one to sleep on, the other to sleep under.

"Am I not to come back, then?" said Quill, staring at the sacks.

"Best not. Col Cane is painting you up to be a rare devil. He has the little ones gathering stones to stone you."

Then the two friends lay on the landing place, sleeves rolled up, reaching into the freezing water to pick little blue crabs off the submerged rock.

Next day Murdo brought a length of horsehair from inside a rope, and they tied it to the bent nail in Quill's pocket, and took it in turns to fish using limpets for bait. Col Cane might have forbidden work, but the outcast demon living in the sea cave could fish and fowl all he liked, seven days a week. Being irretrievably damned had its advantages: a quiet life, birds, and fish-meat (if ever he could catch one).

Each sowing season, after the barley had been sown, the boys and girls on Hirta guarded the rigs against gulls who came looking to steal the grain out of the soil. The stones they threw rarely hit the birds, but even so, what were the gulls doing after all that warranted such unkindness? It was the first time Quill had ever thought of things from a bird's point of view. Perhaps, with living among them, he had turned part bird. Fit for stoning.

9

The Keepers

Next to arrive was Davie, holding a puffin as a peace offering. He laid it just inside the door and enquired, in a businesslike way, if Quill still hated him.

"For what should I hate you, man? For saying I talked to the garefowl? I did. Doesn't make me a witch. 'Twas Col Cane did me that favour."

"You are not a demon."

"I am not."

Davie promptly sat himself down, leaning against Quill's knees. Just as Quill's dog Nettle had done, back home.

Where was Nettle now? Quill wondered. Had the dogs, too, been taken up to Heaven? Or had the world been left awash with cats and dogs and cows and sheep, all abandoned and forlorn now that their owners had been raised to glory? Was Nettle standing on some

Hirta cliff, barking out to sea? She had probably begun rounding up the sheep for plucking, even without the bidding of a shepherd.

"Mine's a good sheepdog," he told Davie. "She knows to take 'em by the throat and throw 'em on their backs."

But when no shepherd came to pluck the fleece, would Nettle bite too deep and turn sheep-killer?

"Truth is, she's a poor herder. Every year she chases one of ours off a high place. We have mutton to eat, but we're running short of sheep."

"I remember!" said Davie. "I had forgot Nettle scaring the sheep. Tell more stories about home."

So Quill told him the story of the Spanish galleon that tried to shelter in the lee of Hirta and wedged itself under a rocky arch and brought it down on top of herself, and sank in the channel along with fifty tons of rock. "And that was what won the war with Spain, because God so loved us Scots that He blew the Spanish fleet all over the ocean and dropped rocks on 'em."

"I don't remember that!" said Davie, astounded that such a dramatic event could have slipped his memory.

"It happened a while back," said Murdo, ducking into the cave carrying a bladder of fulmar oil for Quill to rub on his bruises. "A hundred year. Three hundred? Like as not, you weren't born to see it, Davie."

Then it was Niall who came calling.

Up in Midway Bothy, hearing Davie's garbled retelling of the Armada story, Niall guessed where it had come from and turned up at Lower Bothy, wanting a story of his own. He too had brought a puffin by way of payment.

So Quill told him the story of St Kilda, who was thrown into the sea by pirates, to drown, but spread his plaid on the water where it turned stiff as any raft and, with his shirt for a sail, he sailed to Hirta and discovered it. "He built a huge kirk, but it's gone now, alas, because when St Kilda died, the kirk carried him up to Heaven then turned into a cloud."

There were plenty of cloud spires and palaces to be seen in the sky once Niall started to look.

"I heard St Kilda was a word writ down wrong in a book," said Murdo when Niall had gone. "There was no such man."

"There is now," said Quill.

That evening, he caught his first fish – and then another! It was just a knack, after all. It just called for a little stillness inside. The catches made him hugely happy (for all he loathed the taste of fish); happier still when the garefowl swam up, like a big bandit duck with her masked eyes. He threw her one of the fish. As he watched it slide, lumpy, all the way down her gullet, he felt as if he had somehow made friends with the sea.

The next morning it was John who came, as well as the littler ones. She brought, by way of an entrance fee, a small sack of feathers from one of the cleits. Now Quill would be able to sleep up off the wet, and wake without bruises from the rough floor. Davie said it was Quill's "storytelling chair", and plumped the sack up in the middle of the cave with the kind of reverence he thought due to a throne.

John had stopped with the bleeding, but not with the crying, because now she was sorrowing about her mother. She had woken that morning to thoughts of home, as she always did. But the picture of her mother's face refused to come.

When she said it, Quill saw the boys close their eyes and check inside their eyelids for memories of friends and family: he knew that was what they were doing, because he had just done it himself. Remembered pictures are like water: the harder you try to hold on to them, the more surely they run away. He did not know what to say to John: it is unbearable to lose the memory of a face.

But then Niall up and described John's mother – in perfect detail – just like that – and went on to describe John's grandfather, and their cow Flora, and the clump of wild iris by the door, and the polished boots that stood toe-to-toe with the fireplace, which no one wore except on Sundays. John's mother was instantly restored to her, and even Murdo and Quill were momentarily transported to the fireside of her cottage, coveting those boots.

"I pronounce you 'Keeper of Faces'," Quill joked, remembering Cane's grandiose claim to be Keeper of the Tinderbox. But Niall started, and stared at him as if Quill had just made him Steward of some castellated mansion, its hall's walls covered floor to ceiling with portraits. "Keeper of Faces?" he said, his own thin face memorable for its beaming smile. "Keeper of Faces!"

Once his visitors had gone, scurrying back up the Stac, practising their alibis for being away, Quill tested his own memory, calling to mind all the people on Hirta and all those high above him in Midway Bothy. Apparently the "Minister" now called the boys his "flock". But sheep are all the same: there is no telling them apart. Also, sheep are stupid: will jump off a cliff into the sea sooner than let dogs like Nettle chase them home. And none of the boys was stupid. Murdina had said…

Quilliam stopped short. He could no longer tell whether he remembered Murdina saying things back on Hirta, or if he had imagined them spilling from the beak of the garefowl down by the waterside; or whether the imaginary Murdina had said such-and-such as she lay in his arms at night and they discussed the day, or chose names for their future children…

Murdina had said:

"We all need to be someone, darling, or who are we? Everyone is special for something. Every boy is some manner of a king."

So, Calum he made "Keeper of Music". Calum's voice had broken the previous year and, unlike his clothes, had mended into a marvel of bigness. To look at him, no one would have guessed he had such a voice inside him. He did not altogether believe it himself: Calum was embarrassed to use his new voice. But enthroned on the sack of down – now the "Keepers' Throne" – wearing the title Keeper of Music, and fed with snatches of half-remembered hymns and laments, he swallowed them down then produced a rich, full rendering of each song. Soon it either had the boys in tears or dancing.

John was declared "Keeper of Needles". All the boys had been making needles out of the quills of fulmar feathers, stripping off the vanes and trying to make a hole in the stem with the only knifepoint still sharp enough for the job. The useable ones were going to be precious, Quill said; they needed to be treated with care and stored in a safe place.

The boys' clothes were falling into shreds and, with winter coming, they were going to need more covering, not less. Back in August, they had crammed twenty cleits with sackfuls of bird-down. If now they could somehow quilt their jackets and trews with feathers, they might not – they just might not – die of cold.

"Mam sews a fine seam," said John, as she struggled ham-fistedly to thread a needle with a strand of horsehair.

The Court of King Gannet took a single sobbing breath at the mention of mothers. Niall asked, "What are the mammies doing now, Quill?"

A rocking motion set in among those sewing. Calum, wielding the sharp knife, set it down for fear of cutting himself. Quill had to find some way to lift their spirits. Into his mind flashed an image of Murdina Galloway stepping off the boat, a parcel of old clothes bowling ashore ahead of her.

"You mind that bundle come back from Harris?" he said. "Old Iain's clothes? Well, the wool of the shirts was useless rotten. So the mammies are beating it into felt – a saddle cloth for the grey pony. Even now. On the gutting tables. *Thwack. Thwack. Thwack.* Singing they are. An' look! Suddenly Ma Cane's bat hits something hard. Ma Campbell thinks it's a lump o' grit and goes after it with a needle. But it's not! It's metal, and it shines out the hole, all yellow and glinting. It's a gold piece! An' the more they beat the wool the more it chink-clinks. Old Iain sewed his riches into his shirt, see? And there's four…five – no! – *seven* gold guineas! Ma Farriss starts talking 'bout buying a hat for Sundays with her guinea. But Ma Gillies says, 'Nah, wait, Agnes!

We should put this all by for our boys, for when they get back from the Warrior.'"

Another sobbing communal breath – this time one of exultant delight. Chilly hands closed around the feel of an imaginary gold coin.

Except Lachlan's. "Not mine, won't," he snarled. "My da will have it off her 'fore she can spit."

The rest did not hear: they were too busy sailing with Mr Gilmour to spend their riches on Harris or in some such far-flung land. Momentarily, the End of the World had blinked out of sight, and Hirta was populated again with mothers, fathers and everyday routine. Momentarily, mothers had supplanted angels in the boys' minds, and hopes of home had supplanted hopes of Heavenly rescue.

When Calum brought Quill news that Domhnall Don's raft was almost finished, it felt like proof: that hard work and common sense would carry them home, not whole weeks of Sundays, nor flaming chariots.

All Quill needed of Kenneth was that he stay away. There was a corner in everyone's heart for Kenneth, and it was small, dark and resentful. No one ever shortened Kenneth's name: it took every sharp spike of it to depict the boy's spite. They did not want his company, but of course Kenneth sniffed them out. They could hear him coming a long way off, as he cursed the rock ledges studded with slippery cockles and mussels. He entered Lower Bothy in mid-sentence, badmouthing the "Minister", calling him "a tedious loon". Apparently he had fallen out of favour with Col Cane. Still, this was the great snitcher, who used information like a crowbar to thrash his way through the world. He made an unwelcome visitor.

He looked round at the assembly of boys. Taking the fishing line out of Murdo's hand, he tried his hands at fishing but gave up within a minute. He snatched at a shred of down escaping the story-sack, blew it into the air and tried to keep it there with blowing. Tipping John off the feather-sack, Kenneth picked it up and balanced it on his head, and stood there for some time looking for all the world like a large mushroom. Then suddenly, out of the blue, he murmured, "What will I be Keeper of?"

Quill pretended not to hear, because, frankly, he had no idea what Kenneth could keep. But in the silence that followed, they could smell resentment coming off the bully like the stench off a fur seal. Shoulders up round his ears, Kenneth turned to go, no doubt laden with venom to drop in the "Minister's" ear – the names of all the sinners consorting with the witch Quilliam.

"What day of the week is it, can you tell me?" Quill called as Kenneth ducked out of the mouth of the cave.

A shrug. "Sunday again, 'course."

"But what day do *you* say it is?"

Kenneth gave this serious consideration before shrugging again. "Wednesday?"

And Quill thanked him. "Keep track, will ye? It's rare important someone keeps track o' the day and the date."

And Kenneth turned on Quilliam a smile so ferocious that it showed his bottom teeth. They were gleaming white from chewing on tough, dry bird meat. "I'm 'Keeper of Days', then?" he asked.

"If you're willing. 'S a burden, but it needs someone with a good head on his neck."

Kenneth gave a single nod. It was not a gesture of thanks, but a nod in the direction of the heap of bones. "What's they?" he asked.

Quill gave the most casual shrug he could muster. "Ach, I found a man's carcass far back o' the cave. Reckon it's Fearnach Mor, yes? Washed up again after he drowned." The look on Kenneth's face was worth every puking hour Quill had spent getting rid of the seal's remains.

But at night, curled up on the Keepers' Throne of feathers and covered in a sack, Quill was mobbed by dreams. Vicious as blackbacks, they drove their beaks deep into his head. It was probably the same for the other boys, he told himself. But what did they mean, those violent and terrifying nightmares? He dared not speculate: only witches try to interpret dreams. But he knew they were better out than in – like splinters, or a stone in the boot. Some waking moments found him tearing at his hair as if he might pull off the top of his head and empty out the pictures. His best nights were dreamless. His worst were full of demons and pitchforks; of falling, of ghosts, of a grave chockful of blood-red jellyfish. Whom could he ask to be "Keeper of Dreams"? In whose lap could he dump all those foul night visions to be rid of them?

The day he told the garefowl about them, she plunged into the sea and swam away without touching the precious fish he had laid out for her as an offering.

He told the boys about the garefowl calling on him, but they were slow to believe it. The bird never seemed to lumber past the Bothy when anyone else was there, and they probably thought it was another of his stories. But her visits gave him great joy.

One day she did accept another fish. The next, she even took the fish from his hand, and the day after that she toddled up, swung her head and whacked his fist with her mallet of a beak, as if demanding another treat. Within the week, he woke to find her standing on his chest staring into his face with those white-circled eyes, beak gaping. It was petrifying, and a great hardship to breathe. But long after the heel marks faded from his chest, the feeling remained that he had been done the most immense honour.

He promoted Niall to "Keeper of Memories" so that Niall would sit enthroned on the sack of feathers, asking what memories they had for him to store in his head. One boy's reminiscence would spark off another's: about Hirta, about dead aunts, about fishing trips and Christmases, about dances, heatwaves and blizzards. Soon enough, the cave was a-roar with cries of: "Oh, I had forgot that!" "Man, that was a rare game!" "My da says he remembers when…" "He never did!" "I never heard that before!"

How Niall would keep hold of all the memories, Quill had no idea, but it probably did not matter, not while they perched around the Bothy like so many roosting birds, singing of better days.

Quill thought Murdo would be far too old to be taken in by the daft ruse of dubbing the boys to arrive at: "Keeper of this." "Keeper of that". It kept the others happy, but Murdo would surely see it for what it was: a way to make them feel needed. But after his friend sulked for three solid days, asked for his knife back, and demanded to know who Quilliam thought he was, "handing out titles like the King of England", Quill asked him what was wrong. Murdo bunched his shoulders and declared that he would not stand for *anyone but himself* being "Keeper of Ropes".

Quill said of course not, and told him, "It doesna take the likes of me to tell you what you are already."

"How are you all with the confessing?" Quill asked them one day.

Lachlan spat on the ground. "Cane gives us penances to do: sends us out to sit in the rain. We come here instead."

"Better than catching a fever," said Quill mildly, but inside him his chest cramped up tight with savage loathing for the "Minister". How dare he risk the boys catching lung fever or a quinsy? He wondered what penance Cane would allot himself if he caused a boy's death with his prying nonsense.

"We tell him always the same thing," said John. "We all agreed to. Cane gets so bored hearing it, he sends us away."

"John thought up doing that," said Murdo with a little smile, and patted her on the back. His hand lingered. His eyes looked furtively sideways at her in admiration.

"Sometimes Cane slaps us," said Calum.

"Then we don't go back again," said Lachlan.

"And then what does he do to you?" asked Quill. "For not going."

"He sends us out to sit in the cold."

"And we come here, instead."

Everyone laughed. The pain eased in Quill's chest. Perhaps the tyranny of Col Cane was waning, and they could all soon get back to fowling.

When Kenneth came down to Lower Bothy a second time, he only sat down at the back of the cave and stared at the floor. Once again, he did not try to incite anyone to stone Quill or to throw him in the sea. He simply sat, then left. Not until later did Quill find a snaky coil of horsehair tied to a bent nail where he had been sitting. The gift of a second fishing line. He expected to put it to good use: banishment had made him an excellent angler. But he did not keep the gift long.

"That's just me left, then," said Davie bravely, when next he visited. Just he who was too small and useless to be Keeper of Anything. So Quill took him outside onto the sea terrace – "Let the blue-green men bear witness to this!" – and made a great show of entrusting Davie with one of the fish-hooks. Two would have been a boon, especially with the garefowl coming for her daily feed. But he could spare a mere fish-hook to make Davie happy.

"This, Davie, is the Magic Iron Finger of the Sea. I had it off a selkie I saw sitting combing her hair on the rocks. This Iron Finger beckons to the fishes. None can say no to it. Keep it safe, will you? We may need it yet."

Davie beamed with delight: "Keeper of the Iron Finger".

Quill had not intended to set up in opposition to Col Cane, but he seemed to have done so. One by one, every lad but the pious and obedient Euan had eventually come down to visit Lower Bothy.

Even holy Euan came at last.

He ducked in at the Bothy's entrance, golden hair dark with rain, face pinched with cold. The news he was carrying shamed him almost too much to tell it.

"Mr Don says y'are to come back up, Quilliam. Minister Cane is gone up top."

"Up top? What, *Heaven*?"

"Upper Bothy. To keep vigil. And fast. And pray for us all, night and day. You're to come back up."

Driven to holy wrath (Cane said) by the everlasting noise and disobedience of *sinful boys*, he was decamping to the very peak of the Stac, where he would be closer to God and farther away from their bestial ungodliness. He had taken with him all the egg baskets, most of the remaining sacks, the best knife, and the precious tinderbox.

"Did the men not try and stop him?"

"Mr Don woulda, but his arm is broke just now."

"What!" The news was catastrophic. Quill turned on the others: "Why did nobody tell me?"

But Euan was too caught up in his own sorrows to show much concern. As the Minister's altar boy he had been special. But Cane must surely have seen through to his woeful secret – had somehow found out about Euan's failure to walk on water… What other explanation could there be? Because, instead of Euan, the Minister had taken *John* with him to Upper Bothy.

"*He what? He what? He did what?*" blared Murdo.

Quill laid a restraining hand on his friend. "Did John… Was he willing? John? To go?"

Euan only shrugged. Why (his expression asked) would anyone object to serving God and Minister Cane?

Murdo and Quill looked at one another, the same dire thought in their heads.

"*Did you…?*" they asked each other simultaneously. It should have been funny, the synchronized questions, the identical accusing finger they were pointing. It was not. Each had thought the other capable of betraying John's secret.

"Maybe she told him herself," whispered Quill. "Confessed it, during Confession, maybe?"

But Murdo was too enraged to keep his voice down. "*Shut yer beak. She wouldna! She'd never! Now see what you've done!*"

"What's that, exactly? What have I done?"

The other boys were instantly unnerved. They did not understand what the row was about, but here in the sea cave, drunk on story, memories and song, they had tasted a respite from worry. They did not want their haven spoiled by noisy fright.

10

A Welcome Return

Back went Quill, up to Midway Bothy, the younger boys squabbling behind him over who would carry the soggy sack of feathers – the "Keepers' Throne". In fact they fell into a kind of victory procession – if it is possible to "process" vertically up a slab of tilting rock. Only Murdo outstripped Quilliam.

"Have to get her back," Murdo kept saying. "Hav'ta!"

"John'll not have told Cane that she's a girl. She never would," insisted Quill.

"But some bastard else might've."

"Well, it wasna me and it wasna you, and none else knows." Quill was determined not to be infected by Murdo's panic.

"Cane's guessed, then!"

"G'way, man. That fool? He couldna guess how many ducks make one. Reason he didna take Euan is: Euan puts him in the shade. Euan's…real."

"Real?"

"Aye. Euan's the real thing. He's small fun to be with, but he is a proper wee saint. Cane, he's a charlatan. Wants to be top man, like the Reverend Buchan. But for why? 'Cos he wants to order us about; tell us: 'Tuesdays are Sundays now.' 'Night's day.' 'The moon's made o' cheese.' But he's no *sincere*, get me? Reckon Euan makes him feel small… So he didna take Euan up top; he took someone *useful* is all. To fetch and carry for him."

"But he'll notice now! When there's just the two of them. And her so pretty."

"Nah, man. If John was a pony, that noddy would think she was a sheep."

Quill was, in part, persuading himself, trying to lessen the unease clamping his heart. The idea of Col Cane knowingly carrying a girl off to his stac-top "lair" was… His mind swerved away from it so sharply that his head spun. He told himself that John would simply return to Midway if she felt in danger.

He called a halt, took a rest, shut his eyes, breathed deep, allowing his heart rate to slow. If exile had taught him one thing, it was not to dwell on the unbearable: it only gives you stomach ache.

Not so Murdo. He was so atwitch with rage and outrage that he was climbing too fast, missing handholds on the rock. "I'll get her back. I will. I'll go up there; get her back."

"'*Him*'. '*Him*' not 'her'," breathed Quill, looking round to see who was within earshot. "And slow down, will ya?"

"'S alright for you, man. She's no your girl."

"Nor yours, neither," said Quill, taken aback, "…is she?"

It was startling news to learn that Murdo was destined to marry John.

"Does she know?" asked Quill.

"Not yet. But I have her in my head, y'mind? Like you have Miss Galloway. I built a wall round her. So she's mine now. And I mean to have her back." And all of a sudden, Murdo wilted, from vengeful anger to simple sadness. John had been carried away and, along with her, a great many fondly cherished hopes.

No hail of pebbles greeted Quilliam's return to Midway Bothy. No one covered their nose against the stink of his wickedness. Though only two bird-candles were burning, Midway Bothy was delectably warm in comparison with the water's edge: he could only stand still and enjoy the glimmer of heat on his cheeks. "So how is there fire without the tinderbox?" he asked.

"Good luck, for a time," said Domhnall Don. "And then Lachlan."

For a while, they had kept two flames alive, passing them from the stump of one burned petrel to the wick of the next, with a spare kept alight against mishap. But inevitably, some vandal wind would burst into Midway and, ransacking it for signs of life, blow out both lanterns.

So Lachlan had made it his job to climb to Top Bothy, two petrel-candles looped through his belt, ready-threaded with horsehair wicks. Once there, he begged a light from the "Minister" and fetched it down within the shelter of his jacket.

"Like Prometheus stealing fire from heaven," said Mr Farriss to the wall.

Despite the hardships of the climb, there were others who wished they could take Lachlan's place.

Murdo was so desperate to rescue John that he spoiled his own chances. "Next time, let me go, Maister!" he pleaded. "I'll get the tinderbox if I have to kill yon piddock!"

Mr Don, after weeks of holding his own volatile temper in check, was not about to tolerate temper among the boys. "You shall not, boy. Lay a-hold on yourself and keep a clean tongue in you."

"What is it like up there?" Euan asked Lachlan. "Is there an altar? Do they pray all day?"

Lachlan only shrugged. "He comes out to me. I'm no allowed inta his den."

So Euan went on envisaging some holy sanctuary, and begged to be the one to go up there, next time. He asked as eagerly as if the climb to Upper Bothy was the ladder up to Heaven itself. Clearly he was missing the "Minister" like a lamb separated from its mother. But that gave Don grave doubts that Euan would actually *return* from Upper Bothy if he went there, so he brushed aside the offer, insisting Lachlan was the only man for the job: "*He* is 'Keeper of the Flame' now," murmured Mr Farriss, and glanced in Quill's direction. It was a look that said nothing remained secret on Warrior Stac.

When Quill asked about the broken arm, Domhnall Don made light of it. "Ach, 'twill mend," was all he said. "The raft is finished at least." Still, since Quill had last seen him, Don's face had fallen into unfamiliar creases – channels down which all optimism seemed to have trickled away. While putting the final touches to his raft, he had stepped back onto a clump of seaweed and lost his footing. A simple fall against the jagged hide of the Stac was all it took to snap a bone in his forearm and leave him unable even to make it back unaided to the Bothy, let alone launch and sail the raft.

Mr Farriss was forever checking Don's pulse, the colour of his nails, adjusting the sacking sling… If he had knocked Don down and broken his bones deliberately, he could not have looked more eaten up with guilt. If only he had been there when Don slipped! He might have caught him or scraped away the seaweed!

But Mr Don was not a man who knew what to do with pity. He knew as well as Farriss that if his injury cankered, he would die of gangrene. He was fairly sure that, even if the arm healed, he would never carve another spoon, mend another boat, or knit another tunic. Only by putting such things out of his mind could a man like Domhnall Don survive. So he was not grateful for Farriss's fussing.

The friendship which had united the two men against Col Cane had become less while Quill was gone.

Now, when Don pictured a signal fire burning on Boreray's green mound, he did not picture himself lighting it. Someone else would have to go in his place – aboard *his* raft. "How would you like the job, Quilliam McKinnon?" said Don. "I've had no volunteers for it so far. But someone of us must go – and soon. Good weather will be rare from here on."

It was true. Living at the sea's edge, Quill knew better than most the changing mood of the sea. On most days now the wind swerved and veered continuously, the waves ran in several directions at once, clashing and smashing together into chimneys of spray. Making a crossing – however short – was a fearful prospect. Quill did not leap at the offer, despite the beseeching look in Don's face.

The look on *Euan*'s face was plain as writing. *He* should have gone to Boreray when he had the chance: should have walked there over a flat, calm sea. Any fool with a half pint of faith could have done that, and then the Minister would not have cast him aside…

Quill shifted the battered, moulting Keepers' Throne into the centre of the room. Let it serve its purpose one last time. Let Story come to the rescue one last time. Let Story rescue Euan from the pointless treadmill of self-loathing. After all, Cane was no longer there to damn him or stone him for it.

"There was once – listen up, men, this is true; I had it off my father. This one time the Owner's Steward was on his way to Hirta to collect his rent money, and his boat ran into a shoal of herring – big like no man ever saw before. Herring: slithering on and over each other they were, and so close-packed that the boat stopped dead in the water. The gannets were all about, feasting on the plenty – such a flock as blotted out the sun – diving and skewering and gorging theirselves in the water all around...picture it! Then one gannet – the biggest of 'em all – it misses its fishy mark and plunges *into* the boat and its beak drills clear through the boards and the boat is suddenly full of bird. The wings stretch from side to side like a sail fallen down into the boat. There's men on one side of the beast and there's men on the other, and all of them in fear of their lives 'case the hole lets in water and they sink. But to the joy of all, the gannet's head was stuck so tight in the hole that there was no leak, and it stopped there stuck, all the way to Hirta... After the herring shoal parted, y'mind? Men talked of it their whole lives long. So many herring that a man could walk across them like he was walking a causeway!" Quill leaned back on his elbows. "To my way of thinking, that's what happened with Jesus and his fisherman friends."

Domhnall Don, who had been tasting the greasy cooking water in the pot, gave a splutter that spattered the floor round his feet. The boys urged Quill to go on.

"Jesus made all the herring in the world, am I right? So the herring surely came when He whistled? So when He was on the shore and His friends were out on the sea, He whistled up this huge shoal of herring and walked over the water on their backs – to reach the disciples, yes? (They couldn't see the fish, so they were rare impressed.) And Jesus told Saint Peter to try it too…which Peter did – and managed it, of course! Then the herring said enough was enough and stopped cooperating and Peter started sinking. That would explain why no one else in the world has *ever* been able to walk on water. Not without herring anyway. Or coracles on their feet. Not one saint, even, *ever*."

A handful of younger faces turned to look at Euan, eager with delight. *Of course* he had not been able to walk to Boreray over the waves! There had not been enough herring!

Quill could feel Euan's eyes on him, but did not look round (just in case Euan guessed that the story had been invented especially for his benefit).

Col Cane would have screamed "*Blasphemy!*" and pitched stones at Quilliam for sprinkling a sacred Bible story with Scottish herrings. But the "Minister" had let go the reins of power, hadn't he, and been supplanted by the Storyteller.

"Welcome back, Quilliam," said Domhnall Don wryly.

"I say Quill should be 'Keeper of Stories'." It was the first thing Kenneth had said since the Outcast had returned to Midway Bothy. And it pleased Quill more than he could quite understand.

"I could've fair walked on water when he said that," he told Murdina Galloway as he fell asleep in her imaginary arms that night.

11

King Saul's Trews

Next day, the wind again blew out the candles. So Lachlan climbed the Stac to buy a light from the "Minister". He took with him a string of sand eels Quill had caught in Lower Bothy but been too revolted to eat. As usual, Cane heard him scrambling up the last scarp, and met him on the broad terrace in front of the cave. Cane took the putrefying eels, with a look of disgust, and dropped them on the ground. "You can pay me in labour. Fetch me more rocks to the windbreak."

Piling lumps and shards of rock in front of the cave mouth was bruising and back-breaking work. John helped Lachlan, but spoke not a word – shot him no glances – pulled no conspiratorial faces. Perhaps she had been forbidden to speak to anyone from Lower Down.

On the downward climb, Lachlan's arms were doubly weary from heaving rocks. He needed one hand to nurse the two lit birds inside his jacket. So when a roll of thunder startled him, a twinge of pain went through the muscles of his back, and he fumbled his grip on the birds. Feeling the petrel-candles sliding out of his grasp, he instinctively snatched them close. The belly-oil from one squirted out of its neck and met with the flame glimmering there. A searing heat caught Lachlan under the jaw, then trickled down his chest, riding on droplets of burning oil. His jacket, too, caught fire. He screamed, and, high above, some seabird screamed in reply.

A moment later, teeming rain burst from the sky. It doused him almost immediately, but he was left with a pain, from jaw to navel, that felt as if a strip of skin had been torn off him. He half expected his insides to fall out. What distressed him almost as much was having no lit candle to show for it.

Awkwardly, clumsily, hampered by his broken arm, Mr Don splashed fulmar oil onto the shiny burn: his answer to every ailment, from toothache to coughs and constipation. "I would give you whisky, man, but your ma would skin me for it, so it's as well I have none," he said.

Seizing his chance, Murdo tried volunteering to make the climb in place of Lachlan to beg another light. But he was not quite quick enough with his offer. Little Euan was ahead of him, oddly eager for the perilous climb and for the chance of falling to his death.

With his red-gold hair, blue eyes and patched, feathery clothes, he looked, as he climbed, very like an angel ascending. Lachlan had instructed him in how to carry a lit bird-candle in the lee of his jacket on the way down. But someone should have asked what it was that Euan wanted from the "Minister's" hermitage.

Euan was after forgiveness for his sins and to be taken back as Col Cane's altar boy. He was quite ready (he planned to tell the holy man) to face all the privations of a hermit's life: to fast and pray and freeze and keep silent...

All Euan's well-rehearsed words dropped away as he finally stood in the doorway of Cane's Hermitage.

A shamelessly extravagant number of petrel-candles lit the cave. The remains of a dozen guga meals strewed the floor, along with the best knife the company possessed. There was no altar, unless it was the pile of rocks keeping out the easterly wind. A pair of stuffed, patched and filthy trousers hung from the roof. The Reverend Col Cane lay, asleep and snoring, on a crushed mound of straw egg-carriers and two sacks of feathers. Sharing his body warmth, spine against spine, John lay on the same bed.

Euan's cheeks reddened in the wanton heat of all those candles. His admiration for Cane caught light within his breast and burned to ashes. The so-called "Minister" had *not* left Midway Bothy so as to be closer to God! He had gone for peace and quiet, and to eat more than his fair share, and sleep on feathers, and keep the best tools to himself and share his body warmth with an altar boy who was not Euan – even though Euan had tried to be the best of altar boys and even though *he was the one who had had the vision in the first place.*

Euan picked up the knife and stood over the pompous dictator who had made the End of the World seem like his own idea, and then pretended to be a saintly, selfless man.

Well, Euan knew his Bible better than the sexton ever had. He remembered the Bible story of another cave where the marvellous saintly boy David had tracked down his mortal enemy King Saul and found him asleep, sword by his side. Boy David could have killed the villainous Saul right then and there, as he slept, but, being a saint, chose to leave him a message to the effect: *I was here. I could have killed you. I spared your life.* Picking up the king's sword, he cut the fringe off Saul's cloak.

Using Col Cane's own knife, Euan somehow managed, in his fit of righteous indignation, to saw the legs off the "Minister's" stained, shapeless trousers dangling in the candlelight. Their sewn-in stuffing of warm feathers cascaded to the floor like a macerated angel.

"You cut up his trews?" said Farriss.

"He isna fasting or keeping vigil or denying himself or any such thing!" wailed Euan and described a little of what he had seen. *"And he was sleeping on this big feather bed! With John there beside him."*

Murdo gave a roar like a wounded lion, and sank his head in his hands.

"So I did like Saint David did in the Bible!" said Euan.

"*And you didna take the tinderbox?*" said Domhnall Don, incredulous. "You cut the legs off his trews but you didna think to take the man's tinderbox?"

Euan did not understand: "That would've been stealing, Maister!"

The younger boys (ignorant of their Bible stories) thought it was hilarious that Euan had cut up Col Cane's trousers. But the men were merely appalled at the missed opportunity. Euan's mouth snapped shut in glum silence.

But for his broken arm, Domhnall Don would have climbed to Upper Bothy himself, and laid hands then and there on the fire-lighter. He glared at Mr Farriss when he said it, because he wanted Farriss to go instead. If he could, he would have shaken Farriss like a rug – shaken the Kilda Gloom out of him, the colour back in. But Farriss was limp and sick, his skin pale and waxy, and his thoughts too hard to excrete into words. He had settled, like a burned-out bonfire, his embers dying.

Suddenly, Murdo bawled that he *would gladly go up there and cut Cane's throat for him.* Nobody took him up on the offer. No one but Quill understood why Murdo should be in quite such a passion; why, in the silence that followed, they could hear his teeth grinding with rage.

"*Obà,* man. Be still," said Quill. "We'll both of us go tomorrow."

12

The Crossing

John had climbed to Upper Bothy with the "Minister", fearing the unthinkable, wondering who had whispered her secret to Cane. She had been pleasantly surprised by Cane's notion of the hermit life. She liked her food, and her greatest fear – well, her second greatest fear – had been that Cane would deny himself (and her) the comfort of a daily meal, and only drink bird-broth on Sundays, until they both died of holiness. But John's duties, as his altar boy, proved to consist of fetching birds and feathers from every cleit within twenty chains of the cave, and cooking meals. Cane was a glutton and an idler.

As for her greatest fear, that too abated when Cane continued to call her "lad" and "boy", continued to talk politics and to piss in plain sight of her. In her experience these were not things any man on Hirta would ever do in front of a female. She still wondered why she had been chosen instead of pious little Euan, but soon enough found out. Cane, for all his sermonizing, was a man who liked to do as little work as possible. Strong, agile and fleshy, John's appeal had been that John could fetch and carry, cook and sew, and might not sicken as fast as the skinnier boys.

On the third day, when no clouds snagged on the towering pinnacle of the Stac, John caught a glimpse of far distant Skye. It was a rare and stirring sight, but she did not mention it to Col Cane, who had ordered her only to speak when spoken to. It made for a peaceful, if lonely, existence.

Now, though, the "Minister" was raging.

Waking to find his trousers hacked off at the thighs, Col Cane blamed John. Who else could have done it, after all? Laying about his altar boy with slaps and punches, he ripped the down-stuffed clothes off the wretch's back, so as to deliver the beating so richly deserved. But then, through the red mist of anger, and the snowstorm of flying feathers, he made his second discovery of the day. What three weeks of sleeping back-to-back at night had not told him about John, one violent fit of temper had.

John was not a boy. The person standing before him now, shuddering with cold and fright, was distinctly *not* a boy.

"Unnatural creature! What are you?"

Scurrying after the shreds of her clothes, sobbing bitterly, John looked abjectly guilty – felt it, too. She had felt guilty since birth, after all, for not being a boy.

"Are you a temptress? Sent to tempt me out of the paths of righteousness?"

John made a humming noise that might have been a yes or a no. If she was a temptress, perhaps Cane would banish her from his sight and let her go back down the Stac. There again he might throw her to her death off it like a condemned witch.

"I'm just John Gillies, Maister. I canna help…"

Back on Hirta, Cane had a wife; a ribby little woman whose clothes were all fastened with fish-hooks – not simply her shawl but her skirt and blouse and going-to-kirk cape. Husband and wife rarely embraced. No children had come of the marriage. Cane was hard put now to remember more about her than the fish-hooks and a lingering smell of lye soap. Anyway, she was, in all probability, gone now, taken up to Heaven or down to the other place, for all he cared… And lo! God had presented him with a replacement! His shock abated. His cold fear turned to something much hotter. He watched the girl snatch up the shreds of her clothing, denying the trouser-slashing over and over again, and a new idea clanged in Col Cane's head, louder than the Hirta church bell.

He would marry John, and live like Adam and Eve in the Rock Garden of Eden, away from the men who showed him no respect and the noisy and noisome boys down below who plainly had no souls at all.

Meanwhile, Murdo was setting out on a quest of his own: to rescue John from the clutches of Col Cane or die in the attempt.

Sensing how much love had brightened Quilliam's life, Murdo had wanted very much to follow his example, and would have, if it hadn't been for the entire stock of girls and women getting taken up to Heaven while he was away across the water. Then John's secret had come his way, and with it a wonderful possibility. He could still fall in love with John!

Being both shy and patient, he had not mentioned it to her. But the repulsive news of Cane and John sleeping on the same bed had overturned Murdo's shyness utterly. He was atwitch with battle frenzy. He was a stag bellowing for his stolen hind. He would mount watch on Upper Bothy, he told Quill, and when the chance presented itself, rescue his damsel from her high tower, "For all she's been ruined," he added generously.

"Maybe not 'ruined'," suggested Quill, but offered to come along anyway. Taking a furtive glance at the clouds, he was glad to see the sky clearing, the wind going about. It was turning into a lovely day.

But halfway to Upper Bothy, they sighted two figures descending the scree slope. John was wearing a blanket holed at the neck and cinched in at the waist by a plaited straw belt. It could have been termed a dress. There again, all of them were keeping warm the best way they could contrive. So, had John kept her maidenly secret or not?

She was dragging a bulging sack behind her which bounced so lightly down the rock face that it could only be filled with feathers. Cane was wearing a string of gugas threaded onto horsehair and slung around his neck. This mildly ludicrous figure turned, looked, then bumbled on, gugas bump-bumping, short trousers flapping, John following on behind. Why did she not break away? Why did she not run?

"He's after taking the raft!" said Quill, with sudden insight. "Get back to the Bothy, man! Fetch the rest along!"

Murdo did not so much as slow down. "You fetch 'em," was all he said. Nothing was going to deflect him from his rescue mission.

So Quill turned back and took a laborious diagonal route towards Midway Bothy, carrying the news in clenched teeth: *"Col Cane is taking the raft! John's with him!"*

The company rose as one and followed Quill – a clambering swarm of outrage. Only Domhnall Don was incapable of making the climb down. Nursing his broken arm, he stood in the cave entrance watching them go, and cursing fulsomely.

"John?" called Murdo.

If she heard, she gave no sign of it.

The day was beautiful now: still and crisp with a low sun turning the Stac's wet skirts to silver. The raft was tethered to the large slabs of rock which storms and earthquakes sent slithering down the Stac's flank to pile up at the base. This cove had commended itself to Don for building his raft, since it was almost the closest point to Boreray. The island looked close enough for them to reach out and touch: a wedge of grey rock and emerald green grass. A peppering of gulls floated over it, riding the updraught.

"John, what are you doing?" called Murdo. "Dunna go with him!"

She did not so much as look round.

Cane answered for her. "God has told us to cross over."

"Cross over? Where to? Ay, well, be off. But let John alone. Did you hit her? Have you been hitting her?"

"Always a mouthy boy. You may tell the others that I am risking my life for their sake. For their good. For the greater good. We shall dwell in the Hermit's house on Boreray, and pray for deliverance, as the saintly men did in times gone by."

"John, are you willing?" asked Murdo.

At last John shot him a quick, furtive glance out of bruised eye sockets. The bruises made her eyes unreadable. She looked beyond him, too, and must have seen others climbing down towards the bay. It seemed to spur her to hurry.

"I am," she said. Murdo made a grab for her arm, but she snatched it free and scurried back to help Cane drag the raft to the terrace edge. It havered for a moment, rocking on the brink, then grated noisily into the water, swamping the deck and bobbing up again. A piece or two of carpentry fell off and floated away.

"You'll drown yoursel'!" yelled Murdo. "Let me go in your place!"

John gave a snort. "Fine wife ye'd make for the Minister."

Murdo was dumbstruck. Cane shot him a glance, checking to see if he already knew. "John confessed her womanliness to me and offered to be my helpmeet."

"*Ye didna!*" Murdo looked for her to deny it, and John put on the expression of a haughty beauty who has won the title "Queen of Kilda" and means to queen it over the losers.

"We're to be married on Boreray, Col and me. At the stone pillar. There are sheep there," said the bride, wiping her nose on the back of her hand.

"Sheep? What for? To sing the hymns?" Murdo could not see the importance of sheep to a wedding.

"Sheep. If there's bairns to be born, they must have milk."

"And who shall marry you to each other, can you tell?"

"The Minister, o'course, numpty," and she jumped aboard, shifting the raft out from the shore. She took with her a handful of Cane's jacket, so that he teetered and toppled for a moment before having to step aboard himself. His face was white with fright.

"But you'll not lie with the bastard? Dunna lie wi' him! Sure, y'willna!"

"What, jealous, are ye?" she sneered.

"But you'll signal Hirta, will you?" It was Mr Farriss, first to arrive from Midway.

Cane's lips were firmly clamped between his teeth as he stood in the centre of the raft amid his baggage, and gripped on tightly to the mast. There was something admirable about a man so afraid setting sail regardless.

Boys, arriving breathless after their downward climb, began to shout:

"Wait! Wait!"

"Take us, won't you?"

"I'll pluck sheep for you!"

The thought of sheep, shelter and a clear view of Hirta drew them to the water's edge. But Col Cane took up the makeshift oar – a rotten plank – and clumsily swung it at them. "Keep off! 'S too small! 'Twill carry two and no more!" he yelped. "I've had ma bellyful o' scurvy boys! Get away!"

A wave slopped over the terrace and scattered the boys. Seen close-to, the foaming water was enough to change their minds about making the crossing.

"Sit down, won't you, *a chiall mo chridhe*?" John begged him in tones of purest affection, and took over the oar, fending off would-be passengers from the very back of the raft.

"*But you'll signal for help!*" called Farriss again. "*Swear to it, man! Swear you'll signal home!*"

"Yes, yes, yes," groaned Cane, eyeing every nail in the woodwork, every knothole, every spurting jet of upwelling sea.

"*You're a hoor and a Jezebel, John Gillies!*" bawled Murdo, scarlet faced, and threw a futile clod of seaweed after the bobbing raft. "A hoor and a Jezebel!" The curse seemed to stick in his throat because he began to cough and gag. For John had got to her feet, setting the raft rolling on the swell. She took what looked like an angry pace in Murdo's direction... Then she simply stepped off the edge of the raft, still holding the oar, and disappeared underwater.

She resurfaced a moment later, the paddle thrust out in front of her, arms at full stretch and her feet kicking in a clumsy frenzy. A receding wave carried her farther off. The next brought her closer.

Cane, meanwhile, drifted farther and farther from the shore, eyes wide, hugging the mast as the raft revolved gently on the current and the makeshift sail slapped him in the face. It took him a moment to realize what had happened – a slip? an accident? – but as the boys ashore began to cheer John on, Cane actually let go the mast and crawled towards the edge of the raft. It rolled alarmingly under him. He began to paddle back the way he had come – big splashy slaps of his hands into the water, that left him soaked. The raft did not respond, except that, because of Cane's weight, the lighter end lifted out of the water. Under the raised edge swept a large wave, which pitched the raft back towards the shore. It overshot John and she disappeared under its clutter of sea debris, the paddle sticking out of the water like the fin of a shark. Cane threw himself on his face and began reaching into the water, groping for her, while seawater splashed into his mouth and curses slopped out of it.

The boys on shore began to look about them for stones and pebbles, to claw them up and fling them at Cane, for all the world like boys on the barley rigs, stoning seagulls.

"Have a care for John!" warned Quill, who had felt the smart of pebbles and flints.

Too afraid to get to his feet, the Minister cursed them and all their kin, as he crawled back to the lopsided mast and embraced it tighter than any wife. When John broke surface and began again to swim, frog-legged behind the paddle, he pointed an accusing finger at her and bawled, "May you be strangled wi' your own hair and none pay for your burial, minx!"

Without the paddle he could neither head back for shore nor steer a course. But the current was in favour of

Boreray having him. Smaller and smaller he grew with distance, a smaller and smaller shape against the rugged green backdrop, revolving and revolving and revolving…

They rubbed the cold out of her with an assortment of woollen caps. There were a great many volunteers, once the wet plaid was off her and there was proof incontrovertible that John really was a girl. But she did not make it easy for them, wriggling and howling, hysterical with relief, remembering the fear, the thought of drowning, the possibility that Cane would pull her out of the water again and back aboard the raft.

"My idea! I fixed him! I fixed him, the bastard!" she squealed defiantly, when she had recovered the power of speech. "Said I'd only marry him after we crossed over to Boreray. Was the only way to be rid of him, once he knew!"

So siren temptress John had seduced the Minister into making the crossing – a thing he would probably never have dared do on his own – with the promise of becoming his willing wife. Then she had jumped ship at the last moment, leaving him all the solitude he could wish for. The ocean's icy embrace held no fear to equal the terror of Col Cane for a husband. By the time she had finished her explanation, she had won the admiration of every lad who heard it. Her achievement was more than equal to being King Gannet, and surely gave her a status among the boys that she had never dared hope for. What she did not realize was that their admiration had little to do with her heroic daring, her clever ruse. It had more to do with a glimpse of forbidden places, the touch of an icy breast as they rubbed her dry with their hats. John looked down at her nakedness and it occurred to her that never again would she have to hide her guilty secret.

"Did you at least have away his tinderbox?" was the only question Mr Farriss thrust at John. Whether the child was male or female was of no consequence; without fire they would all freeze in the depths of winter.

"He kept it always about him," she confessed. "I couldna." A universal groan went up.

Back at Midway Bothy, Domhnall Don was a man bereft. All along, he had pictured his raft carrying – if not himself – Farriss and two of the boys over to Boreray; had pictured them putting ashore watched by the sheep whose wool they would pluck to warm them, bedding down in the shepherd's shelter – the underground one when the winter storms came… They would be able to see the smoke rise from the cottages on Hirta…and to signal their own good news in return: that the fowling party on the Stac was living still and waiting patiently for rescue.

Lachlan, Keeper of the Flame, got up and tended gently to the two petrel-candles glimmering on their ledges like holy icons on a church wall. Instead of joining the hue-and-cry to Raft Bay, he had climbed, instead, to Upper Bothy – despite his burns, despite his fatigue – and salvaged the still-burning stumps of two petrel lanterns, fetching them tenderly down again to light the place he thought of as Home.

In the days that followed, he even began speaking to the candle-birds, as someone might to the saints in a stained-glass window – thanking them, bidding them goodnight as, from day to day, one bird burned down to its feet, and Lachlan passed on its flame to the next and the next and the next…

If they ever went out, how would more be relit? What when the last cleit was empty of birds…? It was a question Lachlan never asked himself, for what then would be the need for a Keeper of the Flame?

Col Cane survived the crossing. They knew it from the smell of roasting lamb and the pillar of turf smoke rising. Cane might be a castaway cursed with solitude; his hopes might be dashed of having the last and only woman on earth to himself; but he was eating roast lamb in front of a fire, wearing wool within his shirt, and his view was of home.

"It is a signal, at least," said Domhnall Don several times a day, cradling the agony of his arm, rocking forward and back. "They'll look over from Hirta and see that we are living still."

"If there is anyone left to see it," muttered Farriss. And the boys hissed at him through their teeth, writhing with resentment. At least Cane had offered them Heaven, angels, Judgement Day. At least Don was offering them family and hope. Farriss's only explanation lay in tragedy, in having been utterly forgotten, and in a god who had turned his back and walked away.

13

Words and Silence

Parliament convened in Midway Bothy to discuss the situation.

On Hirta, the Parliament of Elders met every morning but Sundays, the men of the island sitting on benches in The Street, their backs against the walls of the cottages, wearing their tam-o'-shanters. The people of Hirta laboured in the service of the Owner, far off in Harris, and dutifully paid their rent, in eggs, birds, feathers and oil, to the Owner's Steward. But the day-to-day running of the island was decided and organized by Parliament: it set the tasks for the day. Heckled by birds, watched by the women in their doorways, interrupted by toddlers and dogs and an occasional blunder of sheep, Parliament studied the weather and made seasoned judgements according to the colour of the sky, the direction of the wind, the lambs due, the fullness of the cleits and, above all, any omens witnessed, good or bad.

Omens seemed even more important here on Warrior Stac than they had on Hirta.

With Col Cane no longer controlling their waking day, it felt only right to restore Parliament. The older boys were allowed to have their say. No sheep, babies, dogs or ponies disrupted proceedings. They tried to exclude John, on the grounds she was a woman, but she was having none of it.

The first decision they made was to send Murdo and Quilliam to Upper Bothy, to fetch down anything of use that Cane had left behind. Egg baskets, for instance, and storm-petrel-lamps. They were told, too, to watch out for omens. Everyone was to watch out for omens.

Cane had taken the sack of feathers with him to Boreray, but in the middle of the floor, amid the bones of cooked gugas, still lay the under-mattress Col had made himself out of a dozen woven egg baskets, their delicate craftsmanship crushed by Cane's bodyweight into nothing but a pile of chaff. For a moment, the sheer waste brought Quilliam to a standstill.

Also strewing the floor, however, were a great many white slips of paper. Murdo began to gather them up. "Bible bits," he said, and thrust a handful at Quill, partly because Quill had an unaccountable liking for the printed word, but mostly in case a wrecked Bible counted as an omen. Quill shoved as many pages as he could inside his clothing, gathered up a row of petrel-candles, a bladder of oil and another of gannet butter, and steeled himself for the climb down. There were three long, stiff feathers, too – from a sea eagle, maybe.

"Will we take some of this straw for kindling?" asked Murdo. But after pushing a fistful of it inside his shirt, he decided that kindling was not worth the prickling, and they left it. On the return climb, they were startled repeatedly by flickers of white on the Stac wall: more pages from Cane's Bible. Still more escaped from Quill's clothing, like gulls leaving their roosts.

Back at Midway Bothy, John was asked to explain.

"He did this curse thing," she said, as Quill presented crumpled fistfuls of pages to Mr Farriss. "After some numpty came and cut up his trews, he did this damning thing. Bell-book-and-candle, he called it."

"He excommunicated…?" Farriss stopped short of naming Euan.

"What y'do is open the Bible upside down, y'say something spiteful than y'shut the Bible and blow out the candle and ring a bell to make something bad happen to whoever… Dunna know what… But Cane had no bell, so he had me say *'dong dong'* whenever he wagged his finger. And the candle had a poor wick and wouldna light. And he opened the book too wide in his raging, and the stitches broke and the pages spilled out in a great waterfall, and that put him to cursing the trews-slasher even more, because the Reverend Buchan give him that Bible for all he couldna read."

Euan turned white with terror at the idea of being cursed, bell-book-and-candle. However low his opinion of the "Minister" had fallen, Euan believed so powerfully in ritual and ceremony that he feared Cane – bell or no bell – had cut him off from all hope of Heaven.

"Nah. I say the angels ripped the Good Book from his hands," said Quill, "before Cane could do a devilish thing. They are kind that way, angels. Elsewise the curse would've fallen on Cane's own head 'cos of him being not the real thing. Only ministers with reading and numbers can do proper cursing. Y'need a badge. Is that no' right, Mr Don?"

Domhnall Don, apparently roused from the laborious task of putting the loose pages in order one-handed, nodded earnestly. "The Church of Scotland hasna given out one such badge since the days of King Malcolm."

And so the curse of bell, book and candle was lifted, though those spilled pages continued to circle the Stac on a north-easterly wind, seeding the ledges and crags with words. In search of something they could burn to keep warm, the boys went after bird nests, as once they had gone after the birds. And if, while they were out there, a page was found, caught on a clump of dead sea-thrift or fluttering between two stones, it would be brought back and read aloud – like a horoscope – for signs, warnings, encouragement. Hope.

Winter cold arrived. Invisible, it stood at the mouth of the cave: there was no door to keep it out. Cold came in and sat down among them, like one of the blue-green men who lived in the sea, whose very bodies *were* the sea. Cold laid clammy hands on their necks and kidneys, their hands and feet. It twanged on their muscles like a harpist. Their blood slowed, mushy with ice. Their tongues froze to a silence, and in the silence they could hear the waves break far below, one by one, two, three, four, five, six… No! Mustn't count to nine or the Kilda Gloom will…

"Keeper of Memories, what do you have for us?" said Domhnall Don, and Niall could not, for a moment open the sea-chest inside his head to fetch out a reminiscence: its lock was frozen solid.

"My dog Rory is the best ever for puffins," John volunteered. "I put him to a burrow and in he goes, good and deep. The puffins go for him, and bite his fur in their beaks, then out he comes covered in puffins, like clothes pegs, all over everywhere."

"That is a singular dog," said Domhnall Don solemnly.

Talk of the puffins sparked a different memory from Calum. "When my sister was Queen of Kilda, she led the girls' fowling party to Boreray, hunting puffins. All girls. They took 277 in one single day!"

A murmur of admiration ran round the cave, for all the memory had been told a dozen times already.

"If they go again next year," said Niall, "they'll find Col Cane in the Hermit's House, and he'll tell them where we are."

The remark was punished with another blast of icy wind. The rocks in the windbreak shifted and creaked.

"Tell again about the grease pudding and the whale, Quill," said Davie, gibbering with cold. The fish heads and crab legs boiling in the cooking pot bobbed about as if they, too, were eager to hear it.

It broke Quill's train of thought. Murdina had just been asking him to show her the Stone of Knowledge on Hirta. So he had been taking her there on the first day of the moon's quarter, helping her climb up onto the rock, hollowed and smoothed by generations of feet. And as she stood there, her hand resting on the top of his head, the power of second sight had come into her, and she had seen as far as next Easter, and her brown eyes had widened and her fingers tightened in his hair and she said... *You and I, Quill, will surely...*

Then Davie's question broke over him and washed away the scene like a picture scraped in the sand. He extricated his own fingers from his hair and put on his cap. "Tell it yoursel', since you know it," he snapped.

Davie recoiled. Farriss uncurled out of his customary position facing the Bothy wall. Cold filled up the space beside Quill's knees where Davie had been sitting. Quill dipped his head and concentrated on extracting horsehair from one of the ropes. He was making more wicks to thread through petrels, even though there were few petrels left. Keeping busy.

Several boys had outgrown their boots since coming to the Stac. No amount of gannet grease would make the leather stretch or soften enough to fit growing feet. So Murdo passed his to Calum and was left only with his climbing socks. Calum's boots went to Lachlan, and Lachlan gave his to Niall. The exchange played out like a ritual, sombrely, momentously, because a pair of boots is a precious possession and hard to part with. Boots hold the shape of their owners: at the funeral of Euan's father, Quill could remember the widow holding a pair of her husband's shoes, stroking the contours of worn leather as hollow now as her heart.

Kenneth would not part with his boots, preferring to prise upper from sole to make room for his toes. But the rest made the gift freely. No payment was asked. The fowlers simply had it in mind to care for each other, being the only people in the world left to care.

"I never had boots before," said Niall with reverent awe. "Thank you, Lachlan! Thank you!"

Domhnall Don, meanwhile, sat using his left hand to stitch gannet skin over several pairs of ragged, ravelling climbing socks. Keeping busy.

Farriss gave his own boots to Murdo, saying he would not need them any more.

"Keeper of Music," said Murdo, his voice high in his throat. "D'you know that song that goes *Mah daddy left me riches...?*"

And Calum sang, in the large, man's voice he had grown into.

"Mah daddy left me riches fine:
A fishing rod without a line,
A pair of shoes with leather soles
And half a hundred big wee holes..."

Seated beside Murdo, John gave a small squirm of surprise as an arm crept round her waist. She looked down at the errant hand as it spread its fingers across her ribcage. Then she glared at Murdo. The hand withdrew faster than it had come.

John got up and moved to sit on the other side of the cave, next to Kenneth.

"...A whistle and a babby's spoon,
The lamplight of a crescent moon...
A flying-over skein of geese,
The colour red, the whiff of cheese,
The ring of bells, the sound of news,
A herd of unseen faery cows..."

As Keeper of Needles John was struggling to turn some fish-bones into needles, but the delicate spines kept breaking. "Can I be Keeper of some other thing?" she said, throwing them aside in disgust.

"Ya can be Keeper o' this," said Kenneth and pushed her hand between his legs, at which point she discovered well enough a use for a very sharp fish-bone. After sticking one into Kenneth, she moved to sit beside the singer.

"An eye to wink, a mouth to lie
An' wings that never learned to fly.
Mah daddy left me riches fine,

So tell me, maid, shall you be mine?" sang Calum, turning to address the last lines to John, who turned red with embarrassment and groaned loudly.

Murdo, meanwhile, had picked up the crab shells littering the floor and begun surrounding himself with the small, pink carapaces. All eyes were gradually drawn to what he was doing.

Generally, last thing at night, Mr Farriss would dose the boys with fulmar oil, squirting the rust-red liquor directly into each mouth from a gannet gut. It was an all-purpose medicine for aching limbs, coughs, toothache, sprains and nausea. All of these afflicted one or more of the boys. But the thing that afflicted them all, after months on the Stac, was constipation, and the mighty fulmar oil was the only remedy to be had. No one turned it down, that slimy, stinking ooze the colour of old blood. But tonight Murdo served it in eleven crab shells and set one down, reverently, in front of each person in the cave. Then he raised his own between two hands. "Sevenfold blessing to our friends, and the strong rope in time of need!"

The familiar toast made every soul draw a sharp breath. They had said it a hundred times at home in their houses: at Sunday dinners, weddings and christenings, funerals, horse races and sheep-slayings, New Year, Easter and All Saints Day. How had they never thought to say it on Warrior Stac?

"Sevenfold blessings to our friends, and the strong rope in time of need!" they chorused, the words bumping and overlapping as clumsily as eleven men and boys crowded together in a small cave.

In the days that followed, this new ritual became so embedded in the day that they spoke it with one voice. *"Sevenfold blessings to our friends, and the strong rope in time of need!"*

When the birds were all gone, and the fulmar oil had run out, they used rainwater instead.

They shook hands with each other, too, before they slept. After all, Crow Cold had come to roost in Midway Bothy. It pecked holes in the skin of their faces, it stole the feeling from noses and fingertips and ears. It hopped about among their sleeping places, spread its claws on their throats, feeling for heat. And the little winged candles on the ledges, burning down from crown to feet, were too small to drive it away. There was a good chance Crow Cold would one night steal a life or two while they slept.

14

Haunted

Quill dreamed that Murdina asked to climb to the top of Conachair. But a cap of white cloud had draped itself over both Conachair and Oiseval and, as the two of them climbed into its clammy whiteness they were instantly lost. Quill called and called to her: nothing but seagulls answered him.

"*Be careful,* a chiall mo chridhe! *Ye canna fly!*" he shouted and, in panic, began to pluck at the wreathing mist, as he would pluck his sheep for their wool. When he woke he found he had baldified a patch of the cap he rested his head on to sleep.

He also found Murdo's hand over his mouth. "Y'were yaldering of *her*," he hissed.

The clammy cold of his dream persisted despite waking. Warrior Stac was wound in a dense sea mist and any face pushed out-of-doors was instantly a-trickle with water drops. The little ones decided the Stac was being lifted up (like St Kilda's kirk) into the clouds, swore they could feel movement, and clung to the walls for fear a jolt propelled them out of the cave mouth and into empty air. Befuddled by sleep, Quill could not understand how the weather of his dream could have leeched out of his head and filled up the whole Atlantic.

Farriss and Don sat with their hats over their mouths: sickness clings to the water drops of a dank sea mist; it can leave a man with lung fever and a graveyard cough. There was no thought of venturing outside.

An uncanny silence fell, every sound muffled by the fog: it was as if Time itself had stopped. Only the two petrel-candles, burning down from head to foot, marked the passing of the day. At around about noon, one went out, its flame extinguished by the sheer dampness of the air.

The world outside appeared to moan, but it was the sound of a wind suddenly rising. The temperature dropped so low that a rag of mist moved freely into the cave. Like a bolt of cloth it unwound and rewound itself into a column of cold, then took on a shape for all the world resembling a man – ragged white hair, holes for eye sockets, a greatcoat aswirl round its feet. Pieces fell away, like rotting flesh from a carcass. The phantom's breath blew out the second candle.

"'Tis the ghost of Fearnach Mor," said Mr Farriss flatly as he might have said, during lessons, *This is brown kelp. Here is Egypt on the map.*

Chaos exploded. Domhnall Don roared like a lion, a noise that was supposed to mean *Nonsense!* but which only increased the alarm. Children curled themselves into balls. John covered her face with both hands at the same time as starting to run, and banged her head on the roof. Kenneth hurled a puffin at the apparition. The bird passed through it and landed on the back of Calum's neck as he crouched with his forehead pressed to the floor, and made him scream that Mor "had him by the scruff". Murdo laughed hysterically, and Quilliam, in trying to get up, found Davie was clinging to his legs, and fell over on top of him. Lachlan and Niall scurried, on hands and knees, out of the cave, onto the rock shelf outside, like sheep with a sheepdog on their heels.

"Mor died in the sea, y'fools!" said Don with a casual air that was supposed to quell the hysteria. "His spirit's in some petrel now, walking the waves."

But Kenneth waved his hands in frantic denial: *"Nah! Nah! Quill found his bones down below! Head an' all! He's here on the Stac! He's here on the Stac!"*

Quill tried to extricate himself from Davie's grip and to explain about the dead seal, and how he had been spinning Kenneth a line...

And then, in a voice so clarion clear that it filled the cave as ringing fills a bell:

"In the name of Christ Jesus, please go away." The words came from Euan.

Somewhere in the wool-white world outside, a stronger wind sprang up, took the mist in its teeth and shook it to pieces. The noise of the sea returned, steady as breathing. A draught ruffled the boys' damp hair. The apparition spun on its heel...and dissolved in the watery sunlight that was rapidly replacing the fog. Everyone turned to stare at Euan.

"Well?" he said, surprised that no one else had thought of it. "Bible says people should cast out demons. So I did." He made it sound as everyday-ordinary a pastime as washing his hands.

It was not clear, afterwards, just who believed they had seen a ghost and who had simply got caught up in the panic. But no one wanted to cast doubt on Euan's power to cast out demons. The incident of the ghost had finally persuaded him he did not lack for faith. The others might now doubt that the world had ended, but Euan was sure enough for all of them. He was a constant, a shining light, not to be snuffed out. So no one openly discussed whether or not the foggy phantom had been real. Which was a shame.

If they had, it might have come to light earlier that Mr Farriss was a man truly haunted.

"I am going after nests for kindling," Farriss called back, as he moved with brisk efficiency along the cliff face. Gone was the sleepy listlessness, the bleary-eyed blankness of the man. Though his skin was still an unhealthy, porridgy yellow, and his hair a blotchy sepia, the incident with the "ghost" had imbued Mr Farriss with new energy. There was something he urgently wanted to do, and the urgency had woken him up. His seasoned skill on a rock face showed itself now, as he traversed the Stac.

"Alone, Maister?" called Quilliam. "On your own, Maister?" It was hardly unusual for Farriss to go in search of solitude and silence: Quill might not have gone after him – but for the fact that this time Farriss had taken Murdo's rope with him. It was looped about his body as he stepped from ledge to ledge, transferred his grasp from handhold to handhold. There was something about his hurried movements that spurred Quill to keep up: that and the fact the man had no sack with him to hold kindling.

Every furlong or so, Farriss turned and told Quill to head back.

He was making for the Overhang, that lime-slathered fist of rock that jutted out over deep water and was home, in the summer, to a seething gallimaufry of seabirds mating, laying, squabbling and squitting from dawn till dark. He tied off the rope round the base of a misshapen boulder and set about filling his pockets: not with old, infertile eggs, nor with sea thrift or gull feathers or dead chicks, but with stones. With intense concentration, he scoured the ledges for pebbles and shards, cracking fragile platelets of scree into sizes easier to pocket. Beneath him, the white rope hung down into empty space, its kinks and bends easing into a straight, clean line that swung like a bell rope in the wind.

"I've been slitting that rope for horsehair," Quill called. "To make wicks. It needs mending."

"No matter," said Farriss.

Quilliam wanted Domhnall Don to come, with his big, bulky, bluff good sense. He wanted Murdo to turn up demanding his rope back. He wanted his mother there to take hold of Farriss by the ears and shake him and tell him he had barley bran for brains, then hug him to her heart and promise not to tell a soul he was such a numpty.

He wanted Euan there to remind Farriss that suicide is a sin. For he saw Farriss's intention as plainly as if he had spoken it out loud.

"I am going home, Quilliam," said Farriss as he lowered himself over the edge of the Overhang. The white rope stretched. The slits Quill had cut in it, to get at the horsehair, opened like gills.

There was some kind of reasoning at work in the man: Quill tried to put himself inside Farriss's head to understand it. It was a frightening place to be. But yes: it made a kind of sense. To hurl himself into the sea, or from the top of the Stac's peak, would indeed be suicide and a mortal sin. Besides, Farriss might lose courage at the last moment. But this way, the rope would bear the sin of his death.

To string a rope over the rim of an overhang makes it impossible to climb back up without a rope-man to pull you up, bodily. And there are no handholds, no footholds: only the rope to cling to. Eventually, the rope would either break under Farriss's weight or time would simply sap him of his last morsel of strength so that he fell to his death in the water below. The stones were meant to carry him down to the bottom (in case he survived the fall and tried, like Fearnach Mor, to swim for his life). The rest of the company would find nothing but the rope, and would put it down to an accident. Even almighty God might be fooled into thinking no sin had been committed.

But Quilliam was not fooled. Quilliam knew. He had no intention of letting Farriss damn himself by committing suicide, no intention of letting this schoolmaster desert his boys, no intention of standing by and watching a good man die.

Quill equally knew he lacked the physical strength to pull Farriss back up.

He wanted Murdina to tell him he was mistaken: that Farriss really was just going after bird-nests. But no soothing voice spoke inside his head, only the hornet whine of blind terror…

...So Quill, too, lowered himself over the brink and trusted his weight to the white rope. He felt the lambskin sheath stretch. He felt it soak up the sweat from his hands.

"Are you mad, boy?"

"Now nothing bad can happen, Maister. Or it'll take me down too."

Quill would not have put Farriss down as a swearer. It takes an educated man (Quill supposed) to know quite so many oaths. The next two minutes were certainly an education.

Then silence, but for the creaking of the rope as it swung in the wind, chafing, chafing against the base of the boulder. The sea, too, was chafing the base of the Stac. The water beneath them was azure and crystal clear. With the sun smothered by low cloud, there was no dazzle, and they could see as deep down as daylight reached – not to the seabed itself far below, but to arches and plinths of rock under the water. They could almost be seeing a drowned city – some sunken ruin of a previous civilization – a mermaid castle, a citadel of the Amazon Queen. Or home to the blue-green men whose lungs breathe ocean brine, who *are* the ocean brine.

"I can simply let go the rope," said Farriss.

"But then I couldna get back up top," said Quill. "Not anyhow."

A seventh wave slopped extravagantly against the cliff below, and the spray rose upwards, but nowhere near as high as the tail of the white rope.

"Fearnach Mor comes to me in my sleep," said Farriss.

After a moment, Quill said, "Murdina Galloway comes to me in mine."

"She does? She *was* a witch, then." Farriss said it as if he found it sad but interesting: not scandalously wicked, just proof that their dreams were indeed made of the same hellish fabric.

"She is *not* a witch. How could you think it! Your own kin! She's a fine person. I just dream her, that's all."

"I apologize. My wife…my girls…" Farriss said, but stopped. He might share his nightmares, but there were treasures too precious to speak of to anyone at all… Instead he said: "Fearnach Mor comes to me. It was me he came to in the Bothy. Says to me that being Nowhere is better than this place. To be Nothing. To be Nowhere. Better than this."

"He's tempting you to do a wickedness. That's just like him… But Maister, if his ghost is still here on the Stac, he canna tell what it's like to be Nothing or Nowhere, because he's stuck here for good and always, doing the haunting. So what does he know about Nothing and Nowhere? You want to spend forever, the two of you, haunting Warrior Stac?"

"I am not a thief like him. I am not a bad…" But Farriss thought better of justifying himself to the boy whose feet were in his face. "Soon the birds we have in store will be gone – the sea too rough to fish. I willna stay and see you all starve and freeze who were put in my care."

The rope's sheath shifted on its horsehair core, and turned them to face the sea rather than the rock. Beyond the obstacle of Stac Lee, the very rim of Hirta peeped at them: Conachair's summit, the Isle of Soay at one end, Dun at the other. Why had no one come to fetch them home? It was such a little, little distance to have come…

"I was weaving the cloth of a dress. Before we came here. A dress for my wife. She had spun the thread, all ready for me to weave it. But I was slow getting started. I left before I could weave all she needed."

Like gill slits, the splits in the rope's lambskin wrapper gaped. Like gill slits, the clouds opened too, and let fall golden sunlight on the sea. And where it fell, to the north, a shape moved through the ocean.

A whale.

It was vast as a galleon – a fleet of galleons, for – yes! – there was not one but three – four – more! An Armada of whales, ploughing their way south-west. Farriss caught his breath.

"The earth is full of they riches. So is this great wide sea…" He whispered it, as if quoting too loud might scare the whales away.

It was so majestic a sight: so unhurried, so disconnected from time or the puny fragments of dry land that stuck up above water and the punier creatures who clung to them. While the whales stayed within sight, nothing else mattered but watching them cruise south-west towards the emptiness of Ever.

"Whales are a thing I never saw before," breathed Quill. "I heard tell, but I never saw."

"I wish my girls could've..." said Farriss.

"Maybe they did. Maybe even now they're on top of Oiseval, looking out."

"The world's no ended, then? You think?"

"What y'asking me for? I'm the boy. You're the one meant to be giving out with the knowledge." A wisp of horsehair escaping the sheath blew in Quill's face, caught in his lashes, grazed his eyeball. With no rope under his thigh, he could not spare a hand to be rid of it. He was carrying his full bodyweight with his two fists. "Afore I weary, Maister, would you please climb over me? You can get over the rim if you stand on my shoulders. Then you can pull me up."

"You could stand on *my* shoulders," Farriss countered. "You go ahead of me."

"But I couldna pull you up, once I'm on the shelf. Like I said: I'm the boy. You have to go up first... Oh, but you could empty those stones from your pockets, if you would, Maister. Lessen the weight. That would be a kindness."

And miraculously, without bothering to deny the stones were there, Farriss scooped shards, pebbles and lime-encrusted stones from his pockets and dropped them into the sea below, smashing the reflection of two climbers on a white rope. Then he climbed the rope – tried to climb the rope – past the boy clinging to it above him.

To scale a rope hanging close against a rock face is one thing, but to climb a rope dangling free calls for a different kind of effort. Though his eyes were shut, Quill felt every part of the man go by him – head gasping, limbs sinewy as dried bird meat, a missed stone in one of his pockets, the arch under the man's ribcage, hollow from hunger, the joints moving in their sockets.

Able at last to take a turn of rope around his thigh and over one shoulder, Quill settled into a sitting position so as to bear the strain of Farriss standing on his shoulders. The last quick push that lifted the man over the lip of the Overhang must have strained the rope beyond endurance, for Quill heard and felt a loud *crack*.

Every Kilda man is part bird, because he knows how it feels to plummet out of the sky towards the brightness of the sea. He has seen it in his imagination a thousand times over. He has known friends and kin who spent the last moment of their lives making that plunge. But though Quill saw, through his closed lids, the bright flash of scarlet fishes, he opened his eyes to find that the rope had not broken, after all. Farriss was hauling him up. Where he found the superhuman strength to do it, God alone knew. The guilty fear of causing the death of a boy in his care?

Or perhaps the whales had lent him some of their Leviathan strength.

Only as Farriss dragged him over the rim of the Overhang by the back of his jacket did Quill discover the source of the "crack". It had come from within his own shoulder where the delicate epaulette of little bones spread out like the start of wings. It was a painful nuisance on the traverse back to Midway Bothy. But Quill decided to keep it to himself: his friends had troubles enough of their own.

15

Light

Their return to the Bothy went unnoticed. All attention was on Domhnall Don, who was crouching by the wall surrounded by boys lying on their faces or squatting with their knees beside their ears. They were watching him flick a knife against the wall. Lachlan was hard alongside him, holding ready a wisp of straw, a crab shell with oil in it, a clutch of feathers. It was as if the two were trying to coax puffins out of a burrow with a mixture of noise and temptation. What they were actually attempting was to strike a light.

Now and then a spark prickled, and all the boys yelped with triumph, but then it was gone. Don's broken arm was held awkwardly across his chest. The fingers of his good hand were scraped and nicked from catching them against the rock so many times, but he carried on slashing the blade against the wall until the tip snapped off – once, twice, and it was too small to use.

Lachlan fetched his own knife. Seeing Quilliam in the doorway, Lachlan confessed to his terrible crime: "I know, I know! I'm sorry! I let it go out. I'm Keeper of the Flame and I let it go out! But we'll get it back, Quill. Honest, we'll get it back!"

Another spark. Another cry of joy. Another groan of disappointment.

Mr Farriss put his hand to his groin, where he had strained himself in hauling Quill up onto the Overhang. He had rubbed at the injury several times on the return climb to Midway. This time, though, he was simply feeling for his pocket. He brought out a single stone left from earlier. "Try this," he said off-handedly, and shot Quill a warning glance for fear he tell the stone's history.

Don struck knife against stone. A spark jumped: a feather caught, the oil ignited – and there was fire again.

"Thank you, Warrior!" Davie shouted up at the Bothy roof. *"Thank you!"* The others thanked Domhnall Don. Lachlan, Keeper of the Flame, leaned back on his hands and purred with relief. Every boy resolved then and there to practise until he could strike a spark. Some even managed it once or twice.

Within the space of minutes, another spark was struck so bright that it painted their eleven shadows on the back wall of the Bothy. Lightning out at sea.

As soon as wicks had been lit, rainwater flavoured with oil and fish-livers set to warm in Davie's ma's cooking pot, they gathered in the mouth of the cave and watched the electric storm shift listlessly across the ocean. Dark trunks of rain, twigs of lightning: the only trees Kildans lived to see. But such trees!

"Did you spy the whales earlier?" asked Quill, but none of them had. "'The Keeper of the Watch' saw them, did you not, Mr Farriss?"

"I did," said Farriss. *"There is that Leviathan, whom thou hast made to play..."* Then he winced, at the pain in his groin. Or a recent memory, possibly.

Quill's shoulder did not drop. His hand did not lose all its feeling – only in two fingers. His collarbone must only be cracked, rather than broken through and through, and swinging loose. It was not serious, he told himself. It would not be the thing that killed him. But the pain said it was not cheered by this good news. When Quill raised his arm to climb, or turned over in his sleep onto his left side, the pain shouted so loud that it left his ears ringing. One night, he dreamed that his dog Nettle had mistaken him for a sheep and had him by the shoulder and was intent on throwing him off Ruaival Cliff.

The cleits were all but empty. Different boys had been sent to fetch food for the cooking pot, so no one person knew for certain which were emptied and whether any still held bird-meat. All the plucked feathers had been fetched in, in an attempt to raise their sleeping bodies up off the cold rock. They sneezed incessantly and their skin crawled with parasites. Itchy, scabby and sore, their flesh cracked open at the least cause, like crabs whose backs split as they outgrow them. It was as though the boys were outgrowing their skin, for all there was precious little to eat.

In the mouth of the cave, water dripped into the cooking pot incessantly – tick tick tick – as if Time itself was running out, second by unforgiving second. It was the last sound they heard at night, the first on waking. The only respite was when the water in the cave-mouth froze into ice, and then the cold was a worse torment than the tick tick tick.

Kenneth, Keeper of Days, said it was All Saints. He said it with a look on his face that dared anyone to disagree, so that they all knew Kenneth, not the calendar, had decided today was the Feast of All Saints.

"D'ye no mean Christmas?" said John. "All Saints is surely gone by."

"Who's Keeper of Days?" blared Kenneth.

After an initial burst of enthusiasm, he had let his calendar duties slide. On the wall of the Bothy, weeks strayed off in all directions, days were missing for want of ash to write with, whole fortnights omitted for lack of interest. But Kenneth said it was All Saints, for all there was sleet on the ledges, and icicles formed overnight along the lintel of the doorway.

"If the Keeper of Days says it is All Saints, let's have it," said Murdo. "What difference does it make?"

What difference indeed, to boys with nothing to feast on. But the Keeper of Memories annoyingly reminded them of autumn feast-days on Hirta – of dancing and pageants, story-tellings and races. In Kenneth's mind, All Saints was associated with a village feast. Part of him expected a feast, just in return for suggesting the day.

"We canna do feasting, but there could be races," said Quill.

Somewhere high above them in the flank of the Stac, a tiny fissure allowed rain to penetrate the rock and travel, like blood through the Warrior's veins, finally oozing out through the ceiling of Midway Bothy. Each drop immediately split into two and rolled slowly down the walls. Four days after rain, the drops formed faster and more often. Puddles pooled on the floor. Now, in the depth of winter, every day was four-days-after-rain. They had grown to hate that oozing stopper in the rock roof that winked at them, catching the light from the single petrel-candle.

But that day – that so-called "All Saints" – they named each water drop after one of the twelve ponies on Hirta and watched them compete – two at a time – in heats – in race-offs – in the final race for the Festival Championship. They roared themselves so hoarse, cheering on their ponies, that when it came to the singing, the Keeper of Music led a chorus of frogs and sheepdogs croaking, coughing and growling their way through hymns, cradle-songs and ballads.

Quill tried to sing Murdina's song: *The water is wide…* But the net holding his memory had frayed, and holes had opened up that let the words wriggle free and swim away.

The littler boys had to do the dancing. The others were too tall to stand upright in the Bothy. Some whose heads had not reached the ceiling when they arrived now had to bend their knees to avoid cracking their skulls. (Quill's shoulder was glad of the excuse not to dance.)

There was no feast. There was no bonfire. But they made John Queen of the Stac, and using greasy ash from a burned-out petrel, drew a spiky crown on the cave wall over her sleeping place. When she sat up, with her back to the wall, the sketch rested just above her hair.

"Tomorrow, can we have Easter?" asked Davie.

"Sheep brain," said Kenneth. "Easter's not after All Saints."

"No, Christmas comes first, Davie," John explained more gently.

"Who's Keeper of Days?" Kenneth snapped at her. "Christmas is when I say."

Domhnall Don shifted his haunches and moved a stone from behind him as if it had been pressing into his back.

Then he turned onto his stomach to peer into the crevice he had uncovered. He swept out, from behind it, a heap of decaying litter, like leaves blown into the angle of a wall. They were feet – the feet of puffins. Every day since Euan's vision, Don had been pulling one foot from each puffin he ate – one each day – and poking it into the hole: keeping a record of time passing. A secretive pastime since others were supposedly keeping a calendar. But then Don was a cautious man, who trusted himself sooner than other folk.

"Suppose we began to...*fret* around the turn from summer to autumn..." he said, and counted out the wizened, tiny feet like a man counting his savings. Ten mouths counted with him, silently. Ten pairs of eyes watched the riches pile up: the currency of Time. Kenneth counted the days on his calendar, ready to challenge this rival Keeper of Days.

"December. Advent," said Euan as the last webbed foot fell onto the pile. "The Time of Coming. They will come for us now."

But Don had not started his puffin-calendar until the day of Euan's vision – weeks after their arrival on the Stac. "By my reckoning the year has turned already. Some nights this arm keeps me from sleeping. The days dawned earlier this week than last. The year has turned already."

The news was greeted with disbelief. The older boys (who had a fair grasp of time-passing) saw it as a sign that the winter was half gone and they might yet live to see spring and the return of the birds. The younger ones saw only the ice of January and February floating towards them, ready to congeal the blood in their veins.

"Sevenfold blessings to our friends," murmured Farriss. "Is it 1728, then?"

Was it? When Time itself has ended, can one year give way to another and still have a number? Was God's abacus still totting up the years? Or had God himself lost count – of the years, of the days, of the number of souls awaiting collection at the End of All Things?

Parliament convened, but not to decide anything. Truly, Farriss and Don were just struggling after some kind of normality, trying to give the days some shape and purpose. The truth was, the birds were gone from the Stac. The Dead time had come. And though it was not a thing you could say to boys, the fowling party had run out of time. Very soon now, they would starve.

"The thing we should do," said Euan brightly, "is to search for omens."

It was true they had let the practice slide. Back on Hirta they had done it routinely every day. Back when they were expecting angels at any moment, they had watched avidly for signs in the sky, hints among the stars, soul birds hovering or monsters erupting from the sea. When had they stopped looking?

Kenneth said, surly as ever, "I'll look out the door and see a few, shall I? Dunna need to freeze our tails off outside."

Lachlan agreed with him, but it was Euan's idea that carried the vote. Domhnall Don (a man who favoured practical solutions) nodded his approval. "Provided you boys promise to check every cleit you pass on your quest; there may be still one or two that we've missed." He added under his breath, "Birds fill a belly fuller than any omen."

"We could go down to the water and the blue-green men would maybe tell us things to come!" suggested Niall.

"Aye, and while you're there, fill your pockets with crabs and limpets," Don agreed, enthusiastic for the idea of fish soup.

But Farriss said no: "None's to go down by the water in this wind. The swell will be massive."

"I hate crabs," said Lachlan.

"Then you can eat air pie, or find us some birds!" roared Don, and the hand he flexed incessantly (to prove it still had movement) looked very like a crab squirming on its back.

Though Quill's shoulder did not much relish a climb to Upper Bothy, the rest of him thought it the surest route to finding an omen. "Sure to be a page or two o' Cane's Bible caught in some cranny."

Murdo said: "Omens aren't omens if you know where to look for 'em." But Quill did not agree: it was no more than common sense to look for them where they were likely to be. Murdo was not convinced.

As the fowlers spread out across the face of the first precipice, heading their separate ways, Murdo saw a cloud the shape of an anvil – "the exact same shape as an anvil, man!" – and decided he should report back to Mr Don with the omen. Quill suggested Murdo just wanted to get back quick and be out of the wind. They argued.

Increasingly, the two lacked the energy for conversation, for jokes. On a diet of oily soup and ice-fringed, sleepless nights, their goodwill was failing and falling back inside their bodies, unable to reach their eyes to look out, or their mouths to smile, or their throats to speak.

"Do as you like," said Murdo. "I'm going back."

Davie, though, was quick to catch what Murdo let fall. "I'll come with you, Quilliam!" he said. "Where are we going?"

Quill rubbed his shoulder, preoccupied – worried that he might not manage the climb after all. But seeing the eagerness on Davie's face, he could not bring himself to forfeit the boy's admiration.

"We could go fishing down there!" suggested Davie. "I have the Iron Finger safe here, look, and it would maybe beckon in a fish and inside the fish'd be an omen, like in the story."

Quill wondered which story: there had been so many. These days, all he could think, before he fell asleep, was of the hardness of the stone floor under his bad shoulder and the hunger in his stomach. "Tomorrow, maybe, Davie," he said. "Mr Farriss said the swell's too big."

So it was. The sea was flexing its back as though the sea floor was too strewn with rocks to let it rest peacefully. Each unbreaking wave surged many fathoms up the rock face. Still, they should have gone fishing.

Instead, they climbed towards the summit, the wind coming in fits and starts, slapping them in the face, punching them in the kidneys, whipping their long hair into their eyes. Davie looked like a girl, his hair had grown so far below his cap. Quill supposed he looked much the same himself. (Only John had taken the sharp knife to hers, and chopped it short, sooner than encourage Kenneth, Murdo or Calum.)

They passed Mr Farriss standing within an alcove of rock, like a statue in a church wall. Since the business at the Overhang, the Keeper of the Watch had taken his duties in deadly earnest, subjecting himself to hours out-of-doors, watching for omens or whales... They greeted him as they climbed by him, but he was concentrating too hard to acknowledge them.

Only minutes later, the man's voice came from below them: "*Ship! A light! Light a light! A signal!*"

Farriss was hidden from sight by the ragged bulging precipices of the Stac, but they could just catch his bawling over the sound of the wind. Two boys climbing the steep "chest" of the Stac cannot readily turn round to look, cannot turn their backs on the cliff whose ledges and handholds are all that keep them from falling. So not until they reached a broader terrace could Quill and Davie peer out to sea. *"Where? Which direction?"* Quill called, but Farriss was no longer close enough to be heard.

Had there been a light? And if there had, was it a ship's light or wishful thinking? Angel chariots or a knot of white birds? One thing was sure: it was not a signal-fire, because who lights a fire onboard a ship? Then it struck Quill just what Farriss had said: he was to light a signal fire that the ship would see.

"Is it an omen, Quill?" asked Davie.

"Not an omen. It's a ship. We are to signal it!"

Quill lay down on his stomach and yelled over the ledge's rim: "I'll light a fire! I'll light a bonfire!" Then, unwilling to leave Davie on his own, he told the boy to follow behind him.

"But the omen…" said Davie, pointing out to sea.

"Stop your noise and climb, will you."

From deep in his memory had risen up the memory of feathers and egg baskets piled in a heap, like an unlit bonfire: the bed where Cane and John had slept back-to-back.

"Come on, Davie!"
"Where to?"
"To Upper Bothy, course!"

In the cave the feathers were gone, but the crushed egg baskets still lay where they had served Cane as a mattress. Wind had pulled at the heap, but the straw bits still hung together and seemed to be dry. Davie danced about in the cave-mouth, scanning the ocean for any glimpse of a ship.

"Will it be angels, Quill? Will it be angels in that ship?"

Quill dragged all the chaff together into a mound. Then he began striking his own knifeblade against the floor – the wall – trying to strike a spark. He tore off a fish-skin patch that John had lovingly used to quilt his jacket, and pinched out tufts of feathers from inside.

"Quick, Quilliam! It'll be gone!" called Davie.

A spark. Two cries of triumph. Another disappointment. A fire needs a draught if it is to catch light. Quill pushed at the barricade of rocks in the cave-mouth, intended to keep out the wind. The wall gave way one rock at a time – then suddenly, unbalancing him onto his shoulder. His collarbone screamed. The heap of straw-chaff heaved and stirred, and a gust of cold barged its way into the Bothy, as though it had simply been waiting its chance. On and on Quill slashed with his knife, in time with the throbbing pain in his shoulder, not even noticing when a spark finally fell on the wheaten tangle of straw and blackened it. Then suddenly his face filled up with smoke. Another blast of wind lifted the entire mattress clear of the floor. When the gust left the cave, it took with it all the air, and Quill began to cough.

The mattress was scorching, blackening, without a glimmer of fire. It needed air. It needed the wind to blow it into life. As Quill crawled outside on all fours, dragging the mattress behind him, billows of dirty smoke escorted him to the door before swirling back inside again, loth to face the weather. He let go of it in the cave entrance, where it could not help but catch the full force of the wind, and he stumbled away from the choking smoke.

Quill and Davie, standing on the gentle gradient outside the Bothy, hugging each other to keep their balance, were shoved and shouldered by the wind into a clumsy shuffling dance. The shadows behind them danced too…because the mouth of the Bothy had finally filled up with jumping flame. The combustion set the air spinning, so that hundreds of wispy fragments of straw began to swirl round and round and round and round. Here and there, clumps broke free – firebirds soaring into the night.

Night?

It was not night! They had left Midway Bothy immediately after Parliament, and climbed for two, maybe three hours. It was not much past midday. And yet the sky was as dark as late evening. The Stac was roofed over with solid, slate-coloured cloud, as though the citadel of Heaven itself had descended to hover over St Kilda and they were seeing the underside of its foundations.

"We did it, we did it, we did it!" cried Davie, dizzied and entranced by the swirling vortex of straw. They had made a lighthouse of Warrior Stac, casting a beam of light to one quarter of the compass and far out to sea.

16

Storm

Moments. It must have been moments before the puny remains of the egg baskets were all burned and the fire was out. Fearing to walk over the cinders in the cavemouth, they went to plunder the nearest cleit for food. A puffin, perhaps. They deserved a bite of puffin in return for lighting a signal-fire! Battered harder and harder by the wind, though, they were obliged to crouch down on the leeside of the little storage tower. Quill realized they would not be able to climb down again until the wind dropped. Climb down? They could not so much as get back to the cave, the blast was so powerful.

"Storm coming," said Davie above the noise of the blast.

"You could say," shouted Quill. Their heads were not a hand-span apart, and yet they needed to shout. They had to take off their caps sooner than lose them to the wind. It was then that Quill noticed how Davie's hair was bushed out, every strand separate, as though, like an animal, he could bristle his fur. Putting a hand to his own, he felt the crackle: the air was so charged with electricity that their hair was lousy with it.

Momentarily he wondered: was it they who had done it? Rather than attract the attention of a handful of fishermen or a passing frigate, had their bonfire summoned up the storm instead? The sweat seemed to be freezing to a crust on his skin, the wind to be reaching round the cleit, snatching at him, trying to tug him into the open for a fist-fight. The stones of the cleit shifted against one another – but it held its ground, shielding these descendants of the fowlers who had built it years before.

And several saints, too, seemingly.

Because when the boys turned round to set their backs to the tower, they were confronted with a dozen pairs of eyes. Storm petrels were huddling close to the ground: birds who never normally came ashore during the winter. Those little saints who had suffered a fiery death as winged candles in Midway Bothy. "Mother-Mary's-chickens", who hovered over the souls of drowned sailors; "soul birds", who seized on the souls of harsh ships' captains, and ran with them over the wave-tops.

Storm petrels, which sheltered in the lee of ships when storms were coming.

More joined the twelve, shuffling forward across the boys' legs, even standing in their laps. Neither boy moved, except that Davie tilted his head up against

Quill's so that they could hear each other.

"What do they want?" he asked.

"Shelter, same as us."

"Are they an omen, d'you know?"

"'Course. Holy Mary sent them. For supper."

"But I have nothing for them to eat!"

"Davie," said Quill, "you are surely the brightest star in your mother's sky, and I love you dearly, but...*our* supper, not *theirs*." And he realized how long it had been since he laughed.

They grabbed the birds two at a time, with a fowler's quickness of hand that would have put a card-sharp to shame. In trying to wring their necks, Quill's shoulder betrayed him, so he slid the heads under one hip and rolled his weight on to each fragile skull. He felt the blood through his trews, warmer than the rain. They had barely noticed when the rain began, but did not resent it; it only made the birds slower to take off, easier to catch. Within two minutes the two of them had secured supper for all hands, and broth for days to come.

Reasoning that more petrels would be sheltering in the lee of other cleits, they posted the limp bodies into the little stone tower and headed for the next, a little farther from the Bothy.

They were rewarded with the sight of forty more storm-petrels standing like worshippers before an altar, heads drawn down into their bodies.

"Look, Quill! Look!" called Davie and showed the fish-hook held between his knuckles, the quicker to catch hold on the birds and kill them.

A light at sea. A spark. A bonfire spiralling into the sky. And now storm petrels sent like a gift out of the heart of the sea! It was as if omens were falling as heavily as the rain, filling the boys' eye-sockets and shouting in at their ears: *All shall be well, and all shall be well and all manner of thing shall be well...!*

... Except that the storm petrels had taken shelter from something more terrifying than rain or winter's cold, or old wives' tales. They too could read omens – in the cloud, in the sea's unease, in the seething menace out there in the deep Atlantic. Instinct told them a storm was coming that would spin the world like a weathercock.

It broke cover now, snapping the rope horizon that separated sky from sea, plunging and lunging towards St Kilda as if to sink each island and stac to the bed of the ocean. The sea itself, its hide made scaly by the hammering rain, writhed and rose: a dragon – the World-Eater which myth said lay on the seabed with a belly full of fire. Trident lightning jabbed and stabbed at it, but seemed only to goad the dragon to an even greater fury. Though the rain flattened the far wave-tops out at sea, when those waves broke against the Stac, their spray rose hundreds of feet into the air, with a noise like cannon fire. Over on Hirta, the storm would be flaying away the white sand beach, the thatch from the houses, the turf from the mountainsides. There were no longer spaces between lightning and thunderclaps, but one single, incessant concatenation.

On the peak of Warrior Stac, it drowned the rock slopes under cataracts of icy water, washing dead petrels away into the darkness, washing lime-streaked rocks back to blackness. Only when lightning ripped open the sky could Quill and Davie see each other, or where to set foot, to set hand. They dared not attempt to reach the shelter of Upper Bothy, for all it was only a twenty-minute clamber away. They remained crouching behind the cleit, Quill cradling Davie between his knees, Davie cradling the last of the petrels, like tiny wizened babies, in the crook of each arm.

So Quill saw when the boy's small hands opened, like starfish, stark white in the lightning. "I dropped it!" Davie gasped and started to wriggle. "*I dropped the Iron Finger!*"

"No matter."

"*No! No! It's the Iron Finger! It's magic! And I dropped it! I'm the Keeper and I dropped it!*" And he began to pat at the ground round about, panicked, appalled, frantic.

"We'll find it later, man. Stay sheltered."

"*No! No! The rain'll wash it away! I have to find it!*" And Davie crawled away, out of the lee of the little stone turret, searching for a fish-hook, on a mountainside, in the pitch dark.

"*Davie. Here. Now. Get back here!*"

THERE, said the lightning, aiming its fiery wand at Warrior Stac expressly to illuminate a tiny twist of metal on a bare cragtop awash with rain. Davie fell on it with all-consuming joy and picked it up and held it high in a triumphant fist, for Quill to see. His mouth started to shout something.

With the same triumphant glee, the wind picked up Davie – picked him up bodily, high, high into the air so that, for a moment, he appeared to have taken wing: the bird-catcher become a bird. Then it flung him against the Stac. It must have made a great noise: flesh and bone and skull. But from where Quilliam crouched on hands and knees, staring into the renewed dark, the storm's hooting obliterated every sound.

Face down, belly pressed to the rock, ungainly as a seal come ashore, Quill wormed his way across the ground, discovering each dip and rise and crevice without aid of light. Each crackle of lightning he thought had seared the way ahead into his brain, but in the dark that followed, the image decayed and deserted him. At one point he found himself feeling for the far side of a gully only for the next lightning flash to reveal a drop to sheer and sickening nothingness right under his chin.

"I'm coming, Davie! I'm coming, man! Hold still!" he called, but could barely hear his own voice, let alone a reply. The wind filled up his jacket and tugged so hard that he felt almost weightless.

"I'm coming, Davie! Stay where you are!"

His hand fell on a boy's boot. The lightning kept him waiting a long time to show him the boy wearing it.

Davie could not have hit the rock wall face-on. Apart from the blood coming from his nose and mouth, nothing had grazed or crushed his face. His legs were lying at implausible angles to his body, but he had landed in – or slid into – a slight hollow, so that the wolfish wind had not been able to drag him into the open and devour its kill. It could do no more than flick the boy's long hair around his face. The hollow was full of water, though, and Davie's flesh was the temperature of fish on a slab. He must be made warm. He must be got dry. He must be got to shelter. He must be alive. Anything else was unthinkable.

Night had reinforced the storm's cloaking blackness and there were no stars, no moon, flickers of lightning like the ghosts of murderers sharpening their knives. *More omens*, thought Quill with a nauseated, bitter resentment. What good were omens without the wisdom to make sense of them? What good were omens to Davie now?

Lifting the boy's upper body free of the water with his right arm, he reached inside Davie's shirt with his left, but could feel no heartbeat.

"Canna feel with that hand," he told the boy. "Y'know when y'sleep on your arm and lose the feeling? Y'know? I canna feel a thing with that hand."

He took the measure of the storm. The storm was moving westwards, but dragging behind it a wake of rain: unceasing, freezing rain. It was as if it would rain till the world dissolved.

"Between gusts of wind," he instructed Murdina. "We must move him whenever there's a lull." But Murdina was precious little help with the carrying. Davie was such a weight – such an agonizing weight, that even the wind could not manage to lift Quill and hurl him to perdition. He was all for carrying on as far as the Bothy but Murdina said no, she was too weary to go any farther than the first cleit where they had sheltered. Perhaps it was she who felt the pulse below Davie's armpit and pronounced him alive; Quill could not recall. Or perhaps he was fooling himself. But somehow, between them, they managed to lift the boy and lower him into the storage tower with its fishy reek of dried birds. Davie no more filled it than a single fulmar might. His belt broke in the process and let fall two petrels. Quill rent them open and spilled their oil in on top of the boy – not a blessing or even a medicine: although the plumage of the birds was icy, the oil inside was still warm, and Davie needed warmth.

He and Murdina Galloway climbed in beside him, and stayed there all night. All night the wind howled and prowled around the turret, like wolves scenting carrion. Quill dreamed he was in his tomb.

In the morning, he and Murdina were able to carry Davie as far as Upper Bothy. Though the storm was still ramping, the wind had turned sullen and pettish. And there was daylight. The day before, there had been a mattress of straw waiting that would have made a bed. But Quill had burned it, hadn't he? And pushed over the windbreak? Nothing remained but a dark blot on the floor, and scurrying, icy draughts, thanks to his wasteful, stupid bonfire.

Still, the Bothy was occupied.

An army of petrels were huddled *inside* the cave. Mechanically, without thought, Quill went in among them, like a man harvesting carrots, plucking them up, cinching them under his belt, exhorting Davie and Murdina to guard the doorway and turn back any that tried to escape. Exasperated with their lack of help, he stood there himself, swinging and thrashing at them with his jacket. The cave soon whirled with birds as frantically as the fire had done, as frantically as his brain was doing. *"We'll fill your mam's cooking pot tonight, man! Plenty to eat tonight, look!"*

What with birds escaping and birds falling to the floor, the movement within the Bothy finally stilled and, with it, the mayhem in Quilliam's head.

He arranged the dead storm petrels in serried rows, and laid Davie on top of them, for the sake of their body warmth. Both boys were smothered in the oil the birds had spat out in their fright. Quill had no wicks to thread through the birds, no needle to thread them with, no tinderbox to turn them into lamps, but if he had, he would have gone up in flames himself, like a petrel-candle.

The birds beneath Davie's head became suffused with red, as though they were turning into robins. It might have been the rust-coloured oil expressed from their oleaginous little souls, or blood from the back of Davie's head where it had smashed into the rock face. When Quill placed his woollen cap there instead, it too adopted a red rosette, as though Davie had been awarded a prize as he slept.

"I still have it, Quilliam!" Davie opened his eyes. It was the very first sign that he was still living. "I still have the Iron Finger, don't I?" And he opened his palm.

"You do so."

He had been holding it so tightly that the barb was sunk deep into his palm.

"I kept it safe, didn't I?"

"You did so. Well done, man."

"So I can still be Keeper?"

"Till you are a grey old man with a beard to yer knees and you know every fish by both its names."

Davie giggled. "I was thinking…we could maybe use the Finger to beckon a whale to come to us and carry us to Hirta. Just to tend to the dogs, y'mind?"

"Like Jonah in the whale?"

"Only on top. Not inside. Too dark. Some darks I'm brave with, but…"

Quill agreed that the dark inside a whale would test his bravery, too. It was the worst kind of dark – too steeped in stink. But he was aware of another, worse darkness testing Davie's courage to the utmost. The Bothy was dimly dawn-lit now, but for Davie it was still stuffed full of night.

"Just to tend to the dogs, you know?" Davie repeated.

"What, and then must we come back? To the Stac?"

"To wait for the ships, yes," said Davie.

"The ships with the angels in? Ach, man, can we not wait on Hirta for them? Truly we can. We'll light a fire in every grate and keep the chimneys reeking night and morning, so the angels canna help seeing. Do you not think?"

"If Mam has peat enough to spare," said Davie. The only man in his household, he was still worrying about the housekeeping.

Quill set himself the strenuous, bone-destroying task of rebuilding the windbreak he had demolished the night before to let in the draught. Since he had parted with his jacket, to cover Davie, the labour served to keep him warm. And emptied his head of thinking. Better, anyway, to keep busy and look unconcerned than to squat by Davie like a girl, cooing comforts and praying and stroking his hair. That's not what a boy in trouble wants, is it? Not a boy who's wanting to be brave?

At least, for Davie, the ship was coming. Quill had lit a bonfire, so now the ship Farriss had seen would come for certain sure. Belief was pasted thicker on Davie than the oil, blood, grit and rock chippings in his hair. Over the ruins of the horizon, through the valleys between the mountainous waves, white as an albatross, a ship full of angels would come soon to ferry home the fowling party off Warrior Stac.

"Your garefowl fetched the storm. That's the way of garefowl. Mam told me. They fetch in storms." He broke this news to Quilliam gently, apologetically, knowing his friend would be upset by the painful truth and the treachery of birds.

"She's no 'mine'. Just a garefowl is all."

A little outburst of fright, a whimper, a widening of his eyes hinted that Davie had tried to move some joint, some limb and found he could not. "Will you help me to the ship, Quill? When it comes?"

"Me and more. 'Course."

The rain outside hissed its derision. Two boys, impaled on the tip of a giant claw and held up close to the sky for cloud-beasts to squint at? There was no way down.

At the touch of another thought, Davie snatched Quill's wrist fiercely tight, this time in pure terror. "*And you'll not let Kenneth eat me?*"

"*Eat* you?"

"*He said when the food was all gone, he'd cook up the little ones and eat them!*"

"Huish, wee man, huish. That oaf talks through his arse. He'll do no such thing... D'you think any of the others would let him? We all like you far too much... Shall I tell you a thing? When Murdo and I came up here, we found eagle feathers. White-tailed eagle. Tell you what we should do. We should catch a half a dozen, and harness them, and have them fly us to Hirta, first to see the dogs and then out to the white ship."

"We lost a lamb to an eagle last summer," said Davie doubtfully.

"So? They owe us a favour!" said Quill cheerfully, as though the deal with the sea eagles was as good as done.

"Is Miss Galloway here still?" asked Davie.

It jolted the heart almost out of Quill. The rock he was holding clattered over the windbreak and rolled out of the door. The blisters in the heels of his hands burst and wept tears into his palms. "Should I ask her to go?"

"No! I like her. When I was dead – in the tomb, y'know? – she stroked my hair. I pretended she was Mam." Clearly, during the long and terrifying night inside the cleit, Davie had been conscious...semi-conscious...now and then… All along? Quill went and kneeled down by the mattress of little birds. He curled his back, rested his forehead to the stone and let his arms lie flat along the floor.

He implored the Warrior of the Stac to preserve the life of all Kilda men. He prayed to those angels squabbling over their crumpled maps to shift themselves and come to the rescue. He prayed to the soul-birds cushioning Davie's broken back, not to sip the soul from his body as they sipped invisible insects from the sea spray. He prayed to Murdina to come and to remind him of the words of her song about the boats. He prayed to Farriss and Domhnall Don down below, to ignore the rain and climb to Upper Bothy and relieve him of this intolerable vigil. He prayed to God to make him braver – even half as brave as Davie. He prayed to everyone attending Sunday service at the kirk to remember the fowling party they had sent to the Stac and somehow forgotten to fetch home again. He prayed to the ghost of Fearnach Mor to learn pity, and the whales in deep ocean to fetch help.

But only Murdina came.

He sat up, crossed his legs and began to stroke Davie's hair. First he sang:

"The water is deep, I cannot cross o'er,
And neither have I wings to fly.
Give me a boat that will carry two…"

Later he asked, "Would you care for a story?"

"The one 'bout the Owner's Steward and the grease ball?"

"If you'll take my word that it's a true thing and no word of a lie. The Owner's Steward was caught in rough waters and queasy, and he took it into his head to calm the waters with a pudding of gannet grease.

"*'Dunna do it! Dunna do it!*' said the crew.

" '*Dunna do it! Dunna do it, sir!*' said the first mate.

"'*Dunna do it! Dunna do it!*' said the skipper. '*D'you not see what's passing by?*'

"But the Steward thought they only wanted to share out the pudding between them. And he tied the grease-ball to a rope and over the stern with it – *splash*. Oh, and ask me, was the sea calmed?"

"Was it calmed, Quilliam?"

"Smooth as any pond, man. And the boat stopped its pitching. And the fishes came tumbling over themselves to nibble on the grease, and there was fine fishing… But another came too. Another so mighty it made the great sharks look like sprats beside it. It came, and it brought its nose along – *sniff-sniff* – its beady eye and its jaws, wide open. And twelve ton of carcass came behind it, and beyond that a tail the size of the King's anchor! Because a *whale* had smelled that ball of gannet grease and come to eat it up!"

Davie gave a gurgle of a laugh without opening his eyes. His body relaxed and spread a little, his hands turning outwards. The fish-hook was plain to see, embedded in his little palm. Quill went on stroking his hair. "Well, the Steward put on sail and he put on speed and he put on thirty years and his hair turned white with fright! That whale chased him halfway to Orkney before he thought to cut the rope and give the beast its titbit. And do you know? From that day to this the Owner's Steward has never greased his boots, for fear a whale picks up the scent and comes rampaging in at his window."

Beyond the door, the wind shaped the falling rain – shaped and reshaped it into the likeness of giant figures walking by: sailors in their long sea cloaks or women in their blue dresses and red shawls.

Quill pulled the barb of the fish-hook out of Davie's hand. It hurt the boy not at all.

17

Rite

When someone dies on Hirta, the cry goes out throughout the island, and work stops and play stops and all stops, as each person returns home. Everyone is less for the loss.

Quilliam went outside into the rain and raised such a sound as Fearnach Mor must have made when the boat pulled away, abandoning him to his fate. It was not a call, but a noise from longer ago, when no one animal had raised itself up above any other, and men as well as wolves still howled at the moon. Even the rain recognized the sound and stopped.

Down in Midway Bothy, men and boys were at last released to search for the two gone missing in the storm. They scattered across the flanks of the Stac, calling and whistling, as if to fetch wayward sheepdogs to heel. No one had seen the splendorous signal fire blaze its way into the sky – Quill's half-minute triumph.

But Murdo knew where Quill had been heading – to look for Bible pages in Cane's hermitage. So Murdo was first to climb within earshot of Upper Bothy, first to hear the news that Davie was dead.

He started back down then and there.

"Where are y'going, man? Are you no gonna help me?" yelled Quill.

But Murdo had no stomach for seeing, let alone touching a dead boy. And anyway, horror at Davie's death was quickly followed by the thought: it could have been him. If *he* had agreed to climb with Quill to Upper Bothy, then *he* might be the one lying dead on its floor. Blame shifted, for Murdo. It was not the storm but Quilliam who had caused Davie to die.

Quill was way ahead of him. If he had not made Davie a "Keeper", fabricated that foolish game and feathered a spare fish-hook with ridiculous magic, or if he had agreed simply to go fishing for omens, as Davie had suggested… Banishment seemed no more than he deserved.

Kenneth came all the way up to Top Bothy, because he had never seen anyone dead "but old people in their beds". What he saw killed his curiosity. He pretended the sight was not as grisly as he had hoped and, as soon as his eye fell on the birds under the body, began pulling them out and poking their heads under his belt for the downward climb. He could not wait to be gone.

It was Domhnall Don who brought a rope and somehow contrived to lash the body to his back and carry it, as he had carried many injured fowlers before. His broken arm was strapped against his chest to stop him reaching, grasping, pulling with it. So it looked as if he was carrying a baby as well as a child. As he and Quill descended, strange, inchoate noises burst from the man's throat which might have been sorrow or exertion or pain. His face was chiselled stone, so it was impossible to tell.

"Was there a ship, Maister?" pleaded Quill. "D'you think it saw us? D'you think there was a ship?" But Don had stopped believing Farriss's version of events. If there had been a ship, no one else had seen it or, like the whales, it had passed by, oblivious to the castaways. His silence confirmed that Davie's death had been for nothing: to no useful purpose.

Back at Midway, John was asked to supply the customary weeping and wailing required, women being so much better than men at that particular rite. But John had spent so much of her life suppressing a girl's instincts that keening did not come easily to her.

No one stopped Euan from praying loudly and knowledgeably for an hour.

On Hirta, the men would have set about making a shroud or a coffin of some kind – from whatever could be found – a rug, driftwood, a blanket… But where was any such thing to be had on the Stac, here where the living could barely cover themselves against the cold? Quill came up with the idea of coiling a rope round and round and sewing it edge to edge into two scallop-shaped shells – a lidded cradle of soft white leather.

But Murdo, Keeper of Ropes, called Quill a fool with no respect for other people's belongings. The idea was dismissed as a waste of vital equipment.

Custom said they should be out catching one of the family's sheep and killing and roasting it for the funeral feast. And there were no sheep.

"Time enough for that when we get home," said Don. But Quill, knowing how Davie worried about the family finances, blurted out that the loss of a sheep "would be a very great hardship to Davie's mother".

"One of mine, then," snapped Farriss. And crawling over to the body – correctly laid out, washed and blue-white naked – he took Davie in his arms and held him and rocked him and wept, speaking not Davie's name but the names of his two daughters. Everyone looked away.

In the afternoon, the smell of roasting sheep did drift over from Boreray, nicely in accordance with funeral custom. But all that it signified was that Col Cane had survived the storm. The younger boys promptly insisted on a funeral feast of storm petrels cooked in their own oil and, while the meal cooked, they filched items from the pile of Davie's clothing. After all, he did not need them any more.

Euan was still yaldering on about the "sure and certain resurrection of the dead" but nothing on the Stac was sure and certain: only the bitter cold, the hunger, the graze, the bruise, the wind, the sea, and Death.

Fortunately, Calum knew a good many laments to sing after nightfall. Niall, Keeper of Memories, could remember small kindnesses Davie had done on Hirta, and how well he had looked after his mother. Quill added that Davie *his own self* had lit the signal fire – which caused a gasp of genuine admiration. And although Calum struggled to turn this heroic deed into a song, it gave Domhnall Don enough material for a speech. In it, he commended "a fine brave boy" into the keeping of God. There was a general mumbled agreement that God would be delighted to have Davie, and that the angels would rejoice. (Though it was true, neither God nor the angels had made much shift to help so far.)

As Parliament began to discuss what to do with the body, the realization came to Quill that he had left Upper Bothy without ever checking the cave for Bible pages.

Or the sky for sea eagles that might carry a boy home.

Three days they should have mourned, but no one had the heart or stomach for it. So next day Farriss carried the small naked body down to the landing site, and those few who could bear to followed along behind.

Great storms pulp the seaweed around the Stac into a bright orange scum, and the cove was stuffed with it. It gave the illusion of softness, but felt like slime and made it hard for men to keep their footing. So the body was set down hastily, without ceremony, where some seventh wave could lay claim to it. They called it a sailor's burial, though none had ever seen one of those. Euan might have known all the right words, but he had not come. No one thought ill of him for it: he had memories that made him too afraid to go to a cove and watch big waves drag a child's body out to sea.

Quill slithered and slipped his way over to the body, ostensibly to arrange the limbs in a more dignified repose, but in fact to push the bent-nail fish-hook back into the keeping of that rigid little hand. "Sevenfold blessings to our friend Davie, and *the strong rope in time of need*," he said loudly, and threw a look of venomous reproach at Murdo. Davie had needed a rope for his coffin and Murdo had begrudged him one.

"Ropes are for the living, not the dead," said Murdo and, turning his back, started for Midway.

"Come here, will ya, Kenneth?" Quill called out, and though the corpse made him squeamish, Kenneth felt obliged, by the stares of the others, to totter over the orange slime. "See here?" said Quill, pointing to Davie's chest. "Look close." Kenneth squatted down, his face averted from the body. It was easy for Quill to grab the hair on the back of his head and ram Kenneth's head down on to Davie's stomach.

"*Eat, then,*" he hissed. "*Eat, ya piddock.* Said you'd start with the little ones, remember? When the food ran out, remember? You'd start on the little ones. What? You don't recall? *Davie* did. *Davie* remembered it well enough. Died with your words in his head. He kept them by and kept them by, thinking, wondering – when will I wake up with my throat cut and Kenneth carving me into messes? Died fearing you'd cook him and eat his body, laughing boy. You laughing now, Ken? *Take a bite, why don't you?*"

Kenneth broke free, leaving a clump of hair in Quill's hand, and skidded away wiping his face over and over with his sleeve, scrubbing at his mouth, and swearing. The remaining boys who saw it also put their sleeves to their lips, as if they could feel the blue cold of that involuntary kiss.

None but Quill stayed to watch the sea take possession of Davie. It was very cold. For a long time the waves seemed to have no appetite for the boy – only lent him a shroud of orange scum. Then the seventh – or was it the seventeenth? – rose up head-and-shoulders taller than the rest, and washed high up the cliff, sneezing icy spray. It rolled and rolled Davie over, like a looter on a battlefield and, finding nothing of value, threw him onto a clutter of off-shore rocks.

Quill sat down with his back to the cliff. It seemed to him that he had let Davie down too many times already. Since his mother was not there to sit with her boy through two days and nights, then he would do it for her, come hail, come snow, come sea monsters or pounding sea. Let every ninth wave serve him up despair: he had swallowed his fill. Let his friends whisper behind his back:

"*…if it weren't for Quill taking him up to the peak…*"

Let them feast on the petrels he and Davie had harvested, and keep back nothing for tomorrow's hunger. On Hirta they had taken care to eke out supplies, to make them last through the winter months or unforeseen hardship. But here, now, let the last birds be eaten. The last oil had been burned, the sea was too rough to fish with a hand line. So what was the point in putting off the inevitable? They were all bound for the same place as Davie soon enough. It was just that the men chose not to say so in front of the younger boys.

All night he sat there, the cold opening up the seams in his body, as water in cracks swells into ice and breaks off shards of stone. It crept into his head. It bored into his chest. It chewed on his hands. But it could not get the better of him or send him home snivelling to the Bothy. Fever came to his aid and fended off the icy wind with waves of inner heat.

He could not reach Davie's body on the rocks and nor, it seemed, could the sea. At last Night dressed the sea in mourning-black, and hid Davie from sight.

The half-light of dawn arrived, unreal as a dream. The body was gone. Some tide or merrow, or company of blue-green men or white ship had finally stolen closer and accepted the gift. It was as if Davie had never existed. The ragged light flapped in Quill's face, and since hunger had already scuffed holes in his vision, he thought the flicker of white, where the body had lain, was no more than a symptom. Or wishful thinking.

Look, Quilliam. Look! said Murdina out of the tail end of his dreams.

A white soul bird hovers over the body of a good man, so they say. On Hirta, the neighbours would scour the roof ridge of a dying man's cottage, shouting words of comfort in at the window: "*There's a soul bird overhead, Agnes! Your man's soul will rest easy!*" He had seen them shout lies, out of kindness. Or see what they wished was there. Quill would not deceive himself. The birds were gone from the Stac, and Quill did not believe any more in omens.

Look, Quilliam. Look!

Murdina had had no patience with omens or signs either. She had said that people, with God's help, made their own luck. But now she was telling him…

Look to the bird, man! It made no sense. He did not want to look: his head ached and his blood pulsed with heat.

Farriss had called her a witch. And it was true, wasn't it? Quill had conjured her – did conjure her up in the dark and mischievous hours, didn't he? She had filled him with longings he could never live to satisfy. She had bewitched him.

No! You are not looking! Look, Quill!

As the soul departs the body, the soul bird disappears – or so the old-wives' tale goes. Quill's eyes fastened on the flicker of wings, but only to disprove the lie. He refused to believe the bird had come to carry Davie's soul to Heaven. It was just a bird: it would not magically disappear. Besides, it wasn't even white. It was black-and-white. Simply to prove that he was not a fool, he forbade his lids to blink.

Look, Quill! See what's there! But Quill had vowed to resist any new temptations by the sea-witch in his head.

And sure enough, the bird proved him right. It did not disappear. It staggered and keened clear over him, dangling its big feet in his face, then it flapped away and was lost to sight against the cliff above.

What? It did what?

Quill jumped up, slipped on the orange slime and, falling to his hands and knees, scurried – crawled – off the landing place and started up the rock face, already breathless with the effort. Crow Cold must have perched on his chest while he slept, and begun plucking the lights out between his ribs because, yes, breathing was an effort.

Always climbing, clinging on! How long had it been since he walked on the flat? How long since he had walked on turf or sand or dug earth, or set off to run, or straddled a pony? No, just climbing and clinging to the vertical, like a fly on a cottage wall. If ever he got home, he vowed never again to leave the horizontal.

Midway Bothy was strewn with the remains of the eaten petrels. One had been threaded and lit, the better to see by, but it had been allowed to burn out, the Keeper of the Flame falling asleep after his unaccustomed supper. Everyone was asleep. Quill shouted as loud as he knew how.

"*An omen! I saw an omen – but it wasna – an omen, I mean – 'cos it wasna a soul bird…*" He held his ribs, which ached too much to draw breath, and his hands could feel them sucking and blowing like a squeezebox. "*…because it didna disappear, an' it was this near to me – this near, swear to God! – and it was real!*"

They bleared at him sleepily. He wanted to sit down on the soft Keeper's Throne, but Calum was sprawled across it, face down and still asleep. "*Guillies!*" croaked Quill. "*There's guillies coming in!*"

The marks scratched on the wall and Don's hoard of puffin feet both said that February was weeks away yet. The last birds eaten, the last oil burned, the sea too rough…everything said that the fowlers on the Stac were on schedule to starve.

But birds keep a truer calendar. In the autumn, breed by breed, they fly out to sea. Breed by breed, they come back in the spring. And the guillemots are always first, creeping back ashore in the pre-dawn, sneaking aboard dry land like stowaways. Bent on breeding, the guillemots were coming back to the Stac!

18

Spring Fever

The guillemot is a simple bird. It dresses in black and white. It thinks in black and white. Seeing white, it sees – who knows what it sees? – a colony of fellow guillies; a roost that will camouflage it? It looks for white.

The fowlers used the Keeper's Throne, emptying out the feathers – it was only the sack they were after – and set about whitening its fabric with as much bird lime as they could find.

Kenneth wanted to be The Rock, but his feet were paining him where he had prised the uppers off the soles of his shoes and the cold had got to his toes.

Farriss said *he* must be The Rock…but the sack was not big enough to cover a full-grown man. The same went for Murdo now that he had grown to the height of a man. Lachlan said that, now Quill had made him King Gannet, *he* should be The Rock…but even he knew that he could never sit still enough.

Quill wanted the job – after all, the first guillemot had flown over *his* head. But there was fever under his scalp and molten lead inside his lungs and his hands were clumsy and slow; Farriss said he must not leave the cave till he was well. Quill was too feverish to understand: he thought they doubted his word – that the guillemot was nothing but a fantasy – like the ship or Murdina – and that they were not going to go at all. He protested the best he could.

But the task fell to Calum, and it was he who crouched on the Overhang, with only the moon to see by, and pulled the whitened sack over himself and sat as still as – well – as a rock.

"Why did I not think of the sack for Davie's shroud?" thought Quilliam as he fell back into a feverish sleep.

Because it was meant for now, said Murdina inside his head.

The guillemot is a simple bird. It thinks in black and white. And if a man under a white cloth holds as still as stone, bird after bird, returning from a winter at sea, will come cruising in to land on him. Catching them is a magic trick – sleight of hand. As they settle and fold their pied wings, a hand creeps out from under the white cloth and takes one by the throat. The others do not even notice the momentary flutter or the dead bird where, a moment before, there was a live one. They just keep on coming in to land. Who would suppose so many birds could fall for the same trick? But they do.

By the end, Calum was singing at the top of his voice, the notes vibrating with cold.

The guillemots piled up to either side of him had only added to the illusion of a colony and brought more and more birds winging out of the pre-dawn gloom.

Only when the topmost rim of the wintry sun rose out of the sea, did the constant stream of guillemots stop short of the rock and turn away, fearing full daylight would betray them to their enemies. They left without noticing the fifty dead piled to either side of Calum.

So the fowling party would eat again. They could continue to cling to Life as they clung to the Stac, half-guessing they ought to let go, succumb, and escape, as the birds do who fly out to sea and never return to land. And yet the very competitive nature of boys made each of them determined to cling on to life for as long as any of the others: not to be the first to give in. Besides, it was spring, and spring engenders hope in every creature, from the tideline to the mountain peak. Feasting on the guillemots (tough as leather and salty as the sea) their spirits could not help but rise.

The guillemots, too, rejoiced in the spring, barely aware of any deaths at all, so long as it was not their own or their chick's. Life rose up among the wicked blackbacks, too, of course, and the lamb-stealing eagles. Somewhere they too were clattering beaks with some mate who would give them what they most craved: immortality in an egg.

"Ask her," said Quill for the fiftieth time. "Just ask her." But Murdo did not want his advice. Besides, he *was* working himself up to ask John to be his sweetheart, but the time never seemed right.

Kenneth and Parliament took the matter out of his hands.

One day, John was first back to Midway, apart from Kenneth who had been loafing there all day. Kenneth seized her round the waist and made his move: "I'll do the deed with you, if no one else wants to." She punched him in the ear.

In fact, John found Kenneth's wooing so unappealing that she petitioned Parliament to have him stitched into the white sack and thrown in the sea. Despite quite a large vote in favour of this, the sack could not be spared, said Parliament.

Calum remarked affably, "Still, John is fourteen or some such; she *surely* does need a husband."

"I do not. What should I want one of them for?" she protested. "I'm a *boy*. Me mammy says so and it suits me well enough."

"By rights girls canna speak in Parliament," said Euan unhelpfully.

"To my mind…" Lachlan began, "we should check again if she truly is…"

"Ye do not *have* a mind of any sort worth a mention, boy," said Domhnal Don. But Calum was right: at fourteen, John was of marrying age and the question could not be ignored for ever. Should she become betrothed to *someone*, just to settle matters before trouble broke out?

Kenneth, seeing he had blighted his own chances, set out to skewer the chances of his rivals. Niall, he said, was so small and John so big that the boy "couldna climb up high enough, leave alone put an egg in the nest!"

Euan (Kenneth said) was already married to God.

Quill (Kenneth said) had eyes only for the witch Murdina Galloway.

Lachlan (Kenneth said) was such a *bauchle* that his own ma and pa could not find it in them to love him.

Between each insult, Farriss yelled at Kenneth, or Don reached out and slapped at him, but Kenneth only jeered that they were after John themselves and should be ashamed of themselves, them being married men and all.

Niall was, in fact, terrified by the mention of marriage. He could barely even remember to address John as a girl, and still had his doubts that she really was one. Lachlan did offer himself, out of chivalry, but with a look on his face that said arsenic was a tastier idea than getting married.

Kenneth was not wrong about Euan and God; Euan felt no need of Earthly (or earthy) love.

As for Quilliam, the fever had wrapped him in a vaporous vagueness, like smoke. It made him cough, and clouded his thoughts. He tried to fix his attention on the Parliamentary debate, so that he could recount it years from now in a story, but had to abandon the task as hopeless. Let the Keeper of Memories take notes: Niall was much more sharp-eyed and accurate.

Meanwhile, John sat beneath the smudge on the cave wall which had once been her festival crown. Her rough red hands were hidden under her thighs, and she was torn between outrage and excitement at being the focus of attention. From time to time, she flicked her eyes in Quill's direction and smiled wanly.

Murdo wrung his hat between his hands and approached John, stooping, because of the lowness of the roof – which made him look a suitably abject suitor. "I should be honoured, ma'am," he said, which straight away had Kenneth rolling on his back in fits of forced laughter.

"You? You called me a hoor and a Jezebel!" John screeched, and threw a bird's leg bone at Murdo. The words bounced round the cave and the echo caught him in the back of the neck: he had to put a hand to the roof to steady himself. John, recovering her serenity, settled herself back in her place and pointedly asked Quill what *he* was thinking.

"I am thinking, if ever I leave here, I'll travel to the flattest rig of the world where there's never an uphill or a down and the peat goes six shovels deep and winter's two days long. And there are bears. I'd like to see bears. If y'ask me, Murdo is an excellent steady man."

However honest it was, Quill's answer apparently left a lot of important things unsaid as far as John was concerned. She looked down at her lap and sniffed.

Domhnall Don, hoping to get the matter settled quickly, asked John what he hoped were useful questions: "What manner of thing do you like in a man, can you say? A skill with birds? Education? A liking for church and such?"

"What are you asking *her* for?" Kenneth interrupted. "We should take her by turns. I'm on her tonight, Calum the morrow."

Mr Farriss set off across the floor on hands and knees, dog-like in his ferocity. *"You lecherous bullock! I have daughters! John's no a sheep to be tupped! She's Angus Gillies' daughter!"*

But Kenneth was drunk on mischief. "You can watch if you've a mind to, Maister, but you canna play – being a married man 'n' all."

John hugged her knees to her body and buried her face, wishing it made her invisible. A hail of bird bones pelted Kenneth but he seemed impervious. While he could talk dirtier than anyone there, he accounted himself the biggest man among them – the manliest of men – and somehow in charge.

Murdo kicked out at the only part of Kenneth within reach without getting up, but only managed to land a glancing blow to the sole of his boot. To his great satisfaction, Kenneth shrieked like a blackback and went on shrieking, while everyone recoiled from the din, and stared at him, trying to guess what new ploy this was.

But Kenneth did not stop screaming.

Quill, through the haze of fever, heard the sound as if from a mile away, but it came with a smell attached. He was intrigued by the fact that drops of sweat and the drizzle from his nose were all rolling *down* his face and neck, but that the smell was crawling *upwards* – up his nostrils and into his brain, along with images of Soay sheep, their stumpy tails rotting and wormy. "He's rotting," he said. "Kenneth's rotting in the hoof." He was dimly aware that it sounded heartless, but he had no reserves of compassion in his head, only that foul smell and the noise of Kenneth screaming in agony. Besides, he had said it too quietly for anyone to hear. "*Feet. Feet,*" he said more loudly. "'Tis his feet have gone." Then a bout of coughing stopped him saying anything.

It was true. Kenneth's toes had succumbed to frostbite. He fought tooth-and-nail their efforts to take off his boots, calling them thieves (and worse) and sliding himself backwards on his elbows, into the low recesses of the Bothy. But they dragged him out by the ankles and several boys piled on top of him, the younger ones having no idea why, the older ones reminding themselves of old grievances against the bully.

Neither their ignorance nor their malice lasted long. When the boots were off, they could see the morbose, gangrenous state of Kenneth's feet. And when Don fetched out his chipped knife and whetted its short blade against the wall, they felt nothing but horror and sympathy. Don held the sharpened blade in the candle-flame where it turned black with oily soot. Then, obliged to work one-handed, he made a start on sawing the toes from Kenneth's frostbitten feet.

Euan stood by, gabbling a miscellaneous jumble of prayers, before going outside to be sick.

But after the first cut, Don dropped the knife, picked up the toe and threw it across the cave at Farriss. "I've not hands enough. You'll have to do it."

Farriss uncurled at once, the muscles of his face rigid with nausea. But he spewed up no protest or excuses. "I know it," he said. He had been wrestling as hard with his conscience as Kenneth had with his tormentors. Farriss crawled across the floor, took the knife from Domhnall Don, and completed the amputation, salt tears helpfully dropping from his top lip onto the grey putrefaction of Kenneth's feet.

Lachlan thought it might help for the patient to know how the operation was progressing – "That's three, that's four…" – so that Kenneth would see an end in sight: "And six and seven and eight…"

It did not help. Words and noises came from Kenneth like demons from a man possessed – and every bit as haunting. Every boy knew that frostbite might possess him, too, when the Stac was still so often armoured in ice. They too might lose toes, fingers, a nose, an ear…

Quilliam perceived the whole appalling ritual as through a telescope or down a long, dark corridor, and thought that the sweat streaming from his armpits must surely be blood, for he could smell blood too now. He could hear them discussing whether to use the white cloth for bandages – deciding against, on grounds of the birdshit it had been daubed with and the fact that it was still needed to catch guillies. They settled on using Mr Don's sling, his arm-bone being as knit as it was ever going to be. Before bandaging, Farriss used their last drop of fulmar oil to disinfect Kenneth's maimed feet. Euan, returning from the Bothy terrace, saw this and nodded approvingly. "Jesus anointed the feet of his disciples," he said.

"Shut yer mouth, Euan," said John through a bush of greasy hair. "Pick up the bits and throw them out the door."

"I coudna!"

"Then just shut yer mouth," she said, and did the job herself.

They did not return to the subject of marriage that day.

Calum and Murdo continued to know always where John was, and to follow her about, like dogs on heat, but such malnourished, flea-bitten dogs that their pelts itched more than their yearnings. John even felt safe to enjoy the attention. But when, at the next Parliament, the matter was raised again, Domhnall Don cut the discussion short by announcing: "John shall give the matter consideration and deliver us her decision in due course…"

John gave an angry gasp, kneeled up and began scrubbing her Festival Queen crown off the wall.

"…*when we get back to Hirta*," said Don.

And John plumped herself down again in a move so decided and final that her thighs slapped loudly together.

19

Monsters

"Where's Niall?" asked Mr Farriss suddenly.

It did not cause much of a stir the first time he said it: Niall was sure to be back in time for the one meal of the day because he was perpetually hungry.

But when, at dusk, Niall was still not back, Don stood outside the Bothy and bellowed his name. Like scavengers contributing finds to the cooking pot, each boy was asked to supply the last time he had seen Niall and where. It did not help much. The sheer labour of getting through each day had stitched them up inside themselves: they had stopped noticing things.

They searched the ledges and familiar climbs close by Midway Bothy, but when the dark grew too thick, still had not found him. There was nothing they could do but wait till morning.

The search had begun again for flotsam and driftwood that might be used for a second raft. There was a strong possibility that Niall had gone down to the shoreline looking for flotsam. Or they might find the boy in Lower Bothy. Niall knew the route there and would have known to seek shelter there if…if something had prevented him from returning to Midway. Quill clenched his left fist, stretched his arm over his head. His collarbone only ached now when rain was coming or the wind turned easterly. Injuries can heal. Fevers can be ignored if there's a need. Not Davie's kind of injury – not Kenneth's – but Niall's lateness did not necessarily mean he was badly hurt, not badly hurt – not permanently, lastingly, irremediably… Tomorrow morning, as soon as it was light, he would begin searching.

With no more petrel-candles, the night-time cave was pitch black, but Quill had become so familiar with the night sounds that he knew the only person sleeping that night was Kenneth, whose snore was distinctive. Angry, desolate Kenneth: he could sleep now, day upon day, week upon month upon… Perhaps in his dreams he was able to climb again – walk up the hills behind the village – do the deed with every girl on Hirta; Kenneth, who had called Quill Keeper of Stories.

There were no stories left in Quill's head – none that would solace Kenneth, none to explain what had become of Niall. Perhaps the lung fever had melted them or they had blown away as steam.

Where is he, Murdina? Where's Niall? No one answered.

They set off next morning – Farriss, Don and five boys with the one and only good rope. Every one of them had come to the same conclusion:

"I'm for looking down below."

"Quill's Bothy, aye."

"That's where he'll be."

Quill said that, in that case, he would search other coves and stretches of shoreline.

"Nay, lad you shall stay here," said Farriss. "The fever is still on you. And you can look to Kenneth if he needs help."

So the two sat in the cave and listened to the others descending the Stac, calling Niall's name.

Kenneth was lying flat on his back staring up at the roof. Quill thought he was asleep as usual until he said, "They should spread the looking wider."

"They should," Quill agreed. "Could be in Raft Cove. Could be anywhere."

"Go on, then. Look."

And Quill did. He was so afraid for Niall that he reefed in his fever like a sail, and stowed it somewhere under his ribcage where it would warm him as he searched. "You be alright?"

"Just go, will you?"

Outside the cave door he turned the opposite way from the others. Certain ledges offered a wider view of the Stac's flank. So he stayed at a height, resolving to circle the Warrior as far as it was possible to go – look up, look down, be systematic. Still, he expected every minute to hear the sound of rejoicing when the others found Niall safe and well.

The sea quickly washed out any noise but its own. The wind was contrary to the tide, so that the air was full of spray off the wave-tops. As high up as he was, it was raining salt water. Even so, Quill could clearly see the dark shapes of three basking sharks cruising southwards past Stac Lee. His vision blurred before coming back into focus.

What became of sailors washed off the decks of ships, fishermen snatched from shoreline rocks, the bodies of children given into the waves' keeping? Were they swallowed down by such monsters as those sharks down there? Or cast up on foreign shores? Dissolved like salt to savour the oceans? Or were they just rolling in the waves, trodden on by seabirds resting from flight?

With wings of his own, Quill could have circled the Stac in half an hour and seen, with gimlet-sharp birdy eyes, every nook and cranny of every rock face. *Where's Niall, Davie? Is he with you?*

But in the end, it was the garefowl once again who came to his rescue. Down at the waterline, the same solitary shape slip-slapped over a semi-submerged platelet of rock, a live fish flapping in her enormous beak. She swayed from side to side like a drunken sailor, and paused each time a wave showered her with spray. The freakish sight drew him irresistibly down towards the shoreline, though he had not worked this rock face before. (It might not be climbable all the way down.) His hands felt like hand-me-downs that did not fit him properly and did not have much wear left in them. He was instantly tired. Though he wanted to keep the garefowl within eyesight, he had to concentrate fiercely on finding hand and footholds. The next time he paused in climbing and turned back to face the sea, the garefowl had disappeared.

But there was Niall.

He appeared to be simply standing talking to himself. On closer inspection, the lower parts of his legs were sunk in a crack between two flat rocks. Every wave that came ashore welled up through the crevice to bubble around his hips. The biggest waves all but smothered him. One whole day and all night he had stood wedged, like a candle in a bottle, thrashed by the sea every few seconds, watched by a pitiless moon.

He seemed neither surprised nor relieved to see Quill, but then he had been visited by a great many other sights during the course of a day and a night.

"Soon have you out," said Quill.

Niall's hair and clothing were clogged with what looked like congealing food. Perhaps so much salt water had forced its way down Niall's throat that he had retched up a week's meals – though he must have eaten gluttonously if that was true.

"Have you out in the shake of a sheep's tail."

"She wants ma head," said Niall. His voice, though shredded by shouting for help, sounded casual now.

"Well tell her she canna have it... Who does?"

"The witch."

"Witch? What witch? D'you mean Murdina?"

A big wave broke over them both and, though Quill tried to shield Niall, he too was all but knocked off his feet. The boy's skin was as icy cold as Davie's corpse had been, and indeed there was something about Niall that smacked of the Other World. The all-pervading stink though was of fish, not decay.

"Let's have you out of there, shall we?"

"The blue-green men came," said Niall, matter-of-fact for all his teeth were chattering uncontrollably.

"Is that so?"

"I asked would they help me. But they only laughed. Horrible faces, they have, Dadda. Horrible faces up close."

The wave, in subsiding through the cleft, gave a derisive chuckle.

"Were you looking for driftwood, man?" asked Quill, trying to lift the boy bodily out of the cleft. It was like trying to uproot a gravestone: both feet were wedged tight.

"There's a conger lives under the Stac. He wants ma toes, but I have ma boots, don't I? Dadda? I have ma boots. This conger – he got the taste of Kenneth's toes, see, and he liked them so he come back for more, but he'll no have mine, will he? He won't, 'cos I have ma boots." Between gabbled nonsense, Niall's face froze into a rictus grin, lips drawn back off bared white teeth.

Quill lay on his face on the rock shelf and reached down into the cleft to try and free Niall's feet. He had to hold his breath whenever a wave swamped him. Each dousing left a whistling in his ears as if his mended collarbone was a fife playing piercing loud. His own teeth were chattering now. His fingers fumbled upon the bootlaces, but they were tied in a dozen knots that had compacted into stone-hard pellets.

"Are you going?" asked Niall vaguely. It was as if Quill was no more real than the other monsters that had come to jeer and hurl things at this snared boy.

"I'm going nowhere, but I have to find something sharp…" said Quill crawling across the rock shelf in search of some sharp-edged stone. But there was no comprehension in Niall's face. Thoughts and horrors broke over the boy as randomly as the waves.

"Do I have ma head still?" he asked.

What did it mean? The question brought tears to Quill's eyes. Did Niall know, then, that he was mad?

"You have it square on your shoulders, man."

"Yeah! Ma neck's made of iron, see, so she canna get it off me. She canna!"

Niall looked out to sea and Quill followed the line of his gaze. The garefowl was there again, swimming offshore, its beak held high, its mask looking landwards as if anxious to see things end well. He waved his hand – could not help but wave to the bird who had kept him company during his banishment. "Look, Niall. Look! It's my garefowl. You didna believe me when I said she called on me."

And Niall did hear this time, and did look. But his vacant stare into the middle distance was suddenly fearful and focused on the garefowl. "*She wants ma head! Keep her off me, Dadda! She wants ma head! Witch! Go off, ya witch!*" And he began spitting and crossing himself and rocking to and fro as he struggled yet again to heave his feet free. His shins and calves were scraped raw by the rock clamping them.

Quill's fist closed so tightly around the shard he was holding that it cut into his palm. Even if he could get the boy free, how was he going to get Niall back to Midway? He scanned the rock face beetling high above him, in the futile hope of seeing help on its way. All he saw were guillemots mating precariously on a nearby ledge. The Stac itself seemed to sway, as Niall was swaying, to and fro, to and fro. Was it trying to free its feet from the ocean bed? Dizziness and nausea washed through Quilliam.

As he lay on his face and sawed away at the laces of two boots he could not see and could barely even reach, Niall beat on his back with both fists. "Dunna cut off ma toes! The conger will have ya for it! Dunna! I need ma toes! Stop! I hope the conger gets ya! Hope it takes off yer hands, ye *meirleach*!"

To reach the boots, Quill had to stretch so far into the crevice that his face was pressed to the rock. Was there really a conger eel down there? The thready sensations that wrapped themselves around his hands might be boot laces or seaweed, eels or the fingers of the blue-green men tying still more knots. Quill wondered if madness was infectious.

"Soon have ye out. Soon have ye loose," he insisted as the abuse and the waves broke over him.

At last a sharp crack – two! – and a sagging of leather. Rising to his knees through a hail of punches, he wrapped both arms round Niall, pinning the boy's hands to his sides, and pulled him upwards just as a seventh wave broke with prodigious force against them both. They were spilled on to the rock shelf and, as the wave withdrew, Niall broke free using both feet to push the boot-stealer away. Quill slid, on a sheen of water, over the rim of the shelf and into the sea.

Despite the shock of the cold, he somehow kept hold of the ledge with one hand, but as he struggled to pull himself ashore again, Niall lay on his side howling and kicking out at Quill's face. *"You took ma boots! You stole ma boots, ye mearleach! Lachlan gived me those boots!"*

"Niall, let me up. You're free, look! You're out. You're safe, y'donkey. Let me up!"

But somehow, Quill had become the cause of every evil, from the horror of Kenneth's amputation to the number of monsters in the sea. He was a thief, a demon, a cannibal, a blue-green man come to claw Niall out of the breathing world and into deep water. Quill pulled himself to and fro along the rim of the ledge, but Niall was not to be outflanked by a blue-green man. He slapped at Quill's fingers, kicked at his face.

Quill turned and pointed out to sea. "Look, man! Shark! There's a shark coming to eat you up! Run! *Run!*" And Niall looked too.

Plainly the nightmare imaginings rampaging around his skull showed him shark and worse. Despite his torn shins, despite his icy feet, and muscles cramping with cold, he splashed barefoot across the shelf and up the rock face, pursued by invisible demons.

There was a hollowness under the shelf – which was simply a ragged-edged platelet of stone left behind as the waves patiently gnawed away at the base of Warrior Stac. There were no footholds to help Quill up, and Niall had left him one unwelcome gift. The conger eel had squirmed its way out of Niall's head and into his own. He was suddenly convinced that it was there, jaws gaping, its teeth razor-edged, coiling around his legs, deciding just where to sink its first bite – which morsel of him to rip away first...

A wave carried Quill's legs and body under the ledge and sank his head underwater.

What becomes of drowned boys, Murdina?

Their blood is in the spume of whales, Quill.

And his eyes, spangling for want of air, were suddenly filled with the dark enormity of whales spouting silver into a sunny sky.

The backdraught of the waves drew his body out again, and his head broke surface. The sea shoved him painfully up against the shelf and something hit him so hard on the cheekbone that he let go of Warrior Stac.

It was a rope's end. Murdo, in throwing down his rope from high above, had been a little too accurate in his aim.

For a while, they looked at each other from either end of the white rope, Murdo from the ledge, Quill rising and falling on the swell.

"Sorry," called Murdo, laying a hand to his own cheek.

"What for?" said Quilliam. "But I mind there's a conger down below, so if you wouldna take too long in coming down..." His voice barely carried. His throat creaked and croaked. As blood retreats to the body's core in time of danger, the fever had retreated to his lungs and nested there for the summer.

20

Witch Hunt

One day, out of the blue, John chose Calum as her betrothed. She was a Kilda woman, after all, and on as tiny an island as Hirta, choice had never been a big factor. Raised as a boy, she knew how boys (among themselves) talked of girls, approving or discarding them as potential mates, keeping any genuine feelings well hidden, for fear of mockery. Most of them could not hold a romantic thought, even with a bucket to carry it in. Conversationally, Calum might be quiet to the point of dumbness, but at least when he sang the old songs, romance and tenderness poured from his lips. For the sake of that, she could ignore the twist in his nose and the beak scar across his cheek. When they were married, she would have him sing to her every night, insisting on it, like a chick gaping to be fed.

Calum was so gratified that he went and washed the guillemot droppings out of his hair in a rain-filled hollow higher up the Stac. He even washed a few other parts as well. But when he came back, John informed him that the wedding would not actually take place until they were back on Hirta and she had new clothes to wear. At which he shook his long, dripping hair, like a dog, and regretted getting it wet.

Everyone there knew that John would have preferred Quill – apart from Quill himself. But before leaving Hirta to go fowling on the Stac, John had never imagined her betrothal to any boy. And Calum with his singing was better than the prospect of Col Cane punching her nightly. Or Kenneth's idea of sharing.

"What shall I call her?" Calum asked. Out of shyness, he asked the room as a whole. "I canna marry a John."

"You can and you shall," said the bride. "I canna be doing with a new name!" And Calum withdrew the question. Her voice was as shrill as any of the fishwives skinning gannets at the gutting tables on Hirta.

Murdo sat down beside Quill, their quarrel over the rope forgotten. "Lassies, eh?" he said.

"Lassies, aye," Quill agreed.

They celebrated the betrothal with crab racing, riddles, jokes and singing. Then, in a game that had grown up during the days of starvation, each man and boy brought one imaginary course of food to the feast.

"Porridge with milk and eggs."

"Oatcake and cheese and whey."

"Fish heads stuffed with the livers."

"Mutton with sorrel and potatoes!"

"Nettle beer."

Memories from a previous life: luxuries long lost to them, yes. But while everyone could still call them to mind, they still existed. Sometimes even a taste came with the memory.

"We must look to building another raft," said Domhnall Don. "Come summer it will be an easy crossing."

"To Boreray?"

"For a start."

The sap of optimism was rising in their veins. Only Kenneth failed to bring food to the imaginary table. If he had it would have been gall and wormwood to poison the lot of them. For he still blamed them for saving his life by leaving him a cripple.

They were turning into birds. They kept moon time. No more calendars. They measured the passing of time in months, by the wax and wane of the moon: each moon-month, the blink of an eye.

Their clothes were bird-skin and down. Their legs, mangled by scurvy, were mottled and yellow and crusted with sores. They lived in the Present: the Past was past mattering, the Future a shapeless improbability. And yet they had come this far: why should they not persist? – spring, summer, autumn, Dead Time.

They were turning into angels; still patiently devout in their strange, half-pagan religion, they went on waiting for the white ship or angel chariot, Amazon Queen or the drying up of the sea to release them from the Stac. But they could not spare those a great deal of thought. Too much to do. Too much pain to be endured. Too many birds to harvest.

All the white ropes were too dangerously worn for cliff work, the nets were shredded, so boys and men clambered about the slabs and spires of rock with no more advantage over the birds than a little ingenuity. And with no wings, no walking on water, they were more garefowl than shearwater or guillemot. Or were they storm petrels, burning down from head to foot until at last each of their flames went out?

The lone garefowl reappeared… Well, it may have been another, but it had the same peculiarity of being solitary. Sometimes single birds within a flock become disorientated and the compass in their head swings awry, and they strike off from the others, like mystics quitting their old lives to go begging through the world. So the garefowl was there again, wading through the gannet and fulmar colonies, seemingly in search of something that would make sense to it. Murdo came to tell Quill he had seen it, and if his lungs had not been so shot, Quill would have hurried all the way there. Slowly, slowly he made the climb, and saw her, and he was glad of the sight. All day long he followed in her tottering, tick-tock tracks.

Niall, though, took the news differently. He had grown calmer over the weeks. His shins had healed; he had not even succumbed to lung fever. Only at night, in his dreams, did the monsters and blue-green men troop by again, gurning and snapping, licking him with icy, wet tongues, shutting off his breath. He talked about them, but mostly to himself, and rarely took part in conversations going on around him. Even so, hearing the words "garefowl" and "sea-witch", he cried out as if he had been bitten by a rat...and then the bite festered, and feverish hallucinations again took over his every waking moment. "The witch!" he kept saying. "The witch is coming! Keep the witch away! She bites off ma head!"

Quill tried to reassure him, but he was still numbered among the monsters in Niall's dreams. If he came too close, Niall still cowered down – did so now, pushing Quill's face away with the flat of his hands. "You stole my boots!"

So Quill told the others: "I think she tried to help. I think the garefowl tried to feed him – y'know? The birdy way? Puking up food like he was one of her chicks." It seemed as plain as day to him. During his banishment, he had fed the garefowl fish at the mouth of his cave. Now she, in return, had tried to feed the boy trapped in the rock cleft. It was what Murdina would have done. It was what his garefowl would have done.

The boys rucked their lips in blatant disbelief. Birds are birds are birds (except when they are witches or the souls of the malevolent dead).

So naturally he said no more – about the fish offal in Niall's hair and clothes – about seeing the bird watching the rescue like a concerned mother... Unable to speak well of the creature out loud, naturally, Quill found her waiting for him in his dreams.

In his dreams, she rode ashore, stubby wings outspread, within a great transparent wave which set her down in Village Bay. She walked up The Street, past the houses, nodding her big nose at the assembled Parliament, by way of greeting. The island dogs barked at her, but were too daunted to attack and could only watch as she crossed over the rigs, and circled the graveyard, plodding on towards Conachair. She meant to climb to the mountaintop and sleep there, because the place was magic.

When she returned, her beak was full of words, pebble-round words and sharp shards, which she fed to her chicks, who sat on benches in the village schoolroom. The chicks were somehow familiar... When she reached Quill, he too opened his mouth, feeling all the greedy excitement of a hungry chick, waiting for her mouth to dip towards his. Not her beak, but her mouth, and not masked at all, but...

The garefowl took hold of him by the loops of his collarbones and shook him painfully. He woke to find Lachlan leaning over him.

They had taken to doing that – leaving Quilliam to sleep when they went out fowling. Mr Farriss said the lung fever – like the Kilda Gloom – needed time to work its way out of a man.

"We got it. Want to see?" said Lachlan. "We got it! Easy as winking! Calum put the sack over it then Mr Don hit it and then we all hit it and hit it and hit it with a rock 'cos it was talking and saying things, and Euan said if we didn't kill it, it would speak the Devil's Secret Word and damn us all… You shoulda seen us take it down!"

"Leave him be," said Farris sharply, "unless you want to catch his fever."

It is true that Quill, as he sat up, was filled with a hot bile that slopped around in him like the oil in a fulmar. But that was not the lung fever: it was the fear, the sickening foreboding, the horrific realization of what Lachlan was telling him. Looking through the forest of their legs, he saw that they had brought their prize home, too.

The sack lay ragged and ripped, but as plumply puffed up with feathers as when it had been the Keepers' Throne. The whitened hessian was red now with the blood of the garefowl inside. Her huge flippers and lower body stuck out at the bottom.

"I tried to stop them," said Murdo.

"Killed the witch, didn't they?" said Kenneth, peering into Quill's face for a gratifying hint of sorrow. Though his crippled feet had stopped him being there, he was sharing now in the pleasure of knowing the sea-witch had been slaughtered.

"Witch be damned," said Mr Don, who had done his best to stop the boys' descent into savagery and bloodlust. He had only suggested they kill it because its huge stomach was so useful for storing bird-butter. Its skin could be used like leather, and its bones carved into all manner of things. He had pictured a month of pleasant and useful evenings with everyone sitting about in the Bothy sewing shoes or purses or whittling pipes, spoons and thatching pegs.

Then all out of nowhere the words "witch" and "storm-bringer" and "the Devil's Word" had fallen into the mix, and talk of Davie's death and Niall's head being bitten off. A "murderous zeal" was the only way Don found to describe the boys' barbarous hysteria and the way they set about the poor beast, in a frenzy of violence.

He had to admit that the noise coming from the sack had unnerved even him – that jumble of vowels and consonants and snatches of breath. He had hoped a quick blow from him would still both bird and the boys' excitement. But the garefowl has a thick skull and a rugged constitution; this one had taken a lot of killing.

For a good few moments Quill wanted to kill them all: Lachlan with his "good news" face; Niall giggling insanely at the death of his monster whose blood was all over his hands and face; Euan rejoicing in his pious slaughter of an innocent creature. Even Mr Don, who had looked at Quill's friend and seen only a case of useful commodities.

Kenneth ducked his head to look in under Quill's brows, trying to catch him out in tears…

Quill would have punched him but was hampered by that same feeling of falling he had had on the night of Euan's vision. Something, if not the world, had ended. He knew it, with a clear-eyed certainty. That was why all the million birds on the Stac were screaming. He could hear them. Inside his head he could hear them. Nothing was left. Nothing would ever come back – not Davie, not the garefowl, not Niall's wits, not Murdina Galloway, not friendship among this mob of vicious, blackback boys.

"Killed the witch, didn't we?" said Kenneth yet again, numbering himself now among the triumphant witch-hunters.

"More fool you, then. Now there's a witch's curse on all your heads," said Quill and he left the cave.

21

The White Ship

In spring there were eggs to gather. There were seals, too – great slabs of slick grey, strewn about on the landing place like washed-up bodies.

"Lard a fit man with seal fat and he might swim as far as Stac Lee!" said Domhnall Don, everlastingly planning an escape. But it would not be his. His arm had healed with a slight corkscrew twist in it, and its hand trembled like that of an old man. Well, he *was* old. Forty, maybe. Forty-five?

The gannets were sitting with their feet up, resting them on their tough little eggs, for all the world like old men in their armchairs, feet on tuffets. Take one egg, and the mother would simply lay another. So long as life went on. Pretty much every egg would hatch, too. Of course half of the chicks would die within the year. Storms. Starvation. So? Half would survive. So long as life goes on…

Even without friends, life went on. The men still spoke to Quill, but no one else did – not since he had told them they were witch-cursed. They did not stone him or turn him out of the cave, but they avoided him as if he had somehow inherited witchery from his beloved garefowl.

He accepted it. He deserved to be cursed with solitude. Because of his stupid talk of an "Iron Finger", Davie had died thinking a fish-hook mattered enough to get smashed against a cliff. Quill had conjured up Fearnach Mor into Farriss's head. He had fed his friends with stories, and what good were stories to anyone? It had been like feeding glass to dogs. He had even misled the garefowl by feeding her fish so that, in her well-meaning way, she had returned the favour, scared Niall out of his wits and been murdered for her kindness. He had told his friends they were cursed and, worst of all, felt no sorrow at the loss of their company. No man, when he dies, can take a companion on his journey into the dark: so why have any in life?

"I know you now," Farriss said to him one day. "We are kin. We both have black ink for blood." Quill did not know what it meant, but did not dare ask.

Farriss was within his eyeline now, setting puffin snares made from rope fibres. What foolish little creatures puffins were. One puts its leg through a snare. Another puffin, intrigued, comes for a closer look.

I just put my leg through this loop, says the first puffin.

What, like this? says the other. A neighbour passes by and they call out: *Hey,* graidhean! *Could you lend us some help here?* And over comes the neighbour to take a look…

So gullible, so easy to take, and by the dozen. Summer brings such plenty.

Farriss had straightened up. He might simply have been easing his back. He looked up at Quill. There was a question in his face. He nodded towards the sea. And Quill looked, too. There was a blemish on the water.

Half rubbed out by sunlight, something was rounding Stac Lee. Basking sharks, perhaps: several had passed by yesterday. But no, this was not *under* the water but on it: something white. A flock of gannets, then, flying close to the waves, flapping?

All over the Stac, boys were unsettled, like fulmars when blackbacks come ripping out of the sky. They stopped their leisurely hunting, and hunkered down, holding still. Lately, Euan had been talking about the beast with 666 on its forehead, which would come rampaging during the Final Days of the world, eating people up. They pictured a sea monster: of course they did. Their world was built on the sea. Perhaps this was the Great Beast coming now, feather-crested with white and this was the top of its head breaking the surface as it walked across the seabed, scenting sin, scenting souls to eat.

Part of Quill was still waiting for the white ship crewed by angels: the one Davie had been so sure would come. His own doubts had ceased to matter: after Davie died, Quill had felt obliged to put on the boy's hopes and beliefs, as if he had inherited his clothes. Angels were scarcely less frightening than the Great Beast. They too would want to pluck the boys off their nests and carry them away into the sky. As sea eagles steal lambs away from their mother. Quill felt fear but also a surge of bitter resentment that the angels might be coming now, too late for Davie who had wanted and trusted in them so much.

Or perhaps this was just a boat – a simple, single-sailed boat. In which case it was bound to sail on past the Stac, oblivious to the boys marooned there.

Suddenly the boys were all on their feet or clinging to their spires of rock or at the Bothy mouth, waving and shouting. Fifty thousand startled birds funnelled into the sky – a whirling waterspout of birds circling and shrieking as if they too had been awaiting the salvation of a little boat tacking out of the west.

In the end, there was no time to fetch anything, anything at all. The boys moved like tethered goats, setting off for the landing place only to be pulled up short by the thought of things it was unthinkable to leave behind: Davie's mam's cooking pot – a woollen cap – the new stock of petrel- candles – a crown daubed on to a cave wall… Half the cleits were full. There was fulmar oil, and bird-butter stored in the gut of a garefowl. There were feathers, too, though not a single sack left for carrying them down to the boat...

But what if the boat could not manage to touch shore? An awkward current, a heavy swell... The wind might move round! An inexperienced skipper might decide not to risk his boat attempting a landing...

Domhnall Don had started to help Kenneth down from the Bothy, along the ledges, down the shallowest slopes of the Stac. The two of them were linked by a tail of grubby rope, in case Kenneth could not keep his balance on his maimed feet. The impression was of a shepherd leading an elderly sheepdog, or a prisoner being led away to justice.

Only Lachlan, balanced high on a spur of rock, stood perfectly still – King Gannet overseeing his sunlit realm. His arms were crossed, and his face turned away every time someone beckoned him to come. Quill had to make a detour to fetch him down.

"I'm staying," he said, and the scowl line in Lachlan's sunburned forehead was so deep it might have been cut with an axe.

"But your people..." said Quill, because what else needed saying? The waiting was over. The world was not ended! They had been wintering at sea for nine months, but now they could get back to the warm jostle of their fellow creatures, their breed, their kin.

"Hope they're dead," said Lachlan brutally, and then, fearing he might be misunderstood, hastily added, "Mine, not yours, yes? Mine, not yours."

It was not the Hirta boat, nor Mr Gilmour come from Harris with post and supplies. It was the Owner's Steward, calling at Hirta to collect the rents. Arriving there, he had been told of the fowling party stranded on the Stac and had come to rescue them. He mentioned seeing smoke on the way over, coming from Boreray. They in turn mentioned the existence of Col Cane.

Cane was standing, ready and waiting, in the cove when the boat put in there, too. Rounding the southern side of Boreray they could see the many futile attempts Cane had made to signal Hirta: white rocks embedded in the grass-green cliff: writing in the alphabet of desperation. He had signalled, after all.

Still, no one spoke a word to the "Minister" – the "Hermit". And though Cane bombarded them with questions, neither the Steward nor his crew were prepared to talk about what they had found on Hirta. "Illness," was all they said. "Sickness."

There was no point in asking the Steward about particular people: the man knew Reverend Buchan's name but that's about all. In truth, the Steward could barely recognize the fowling party as human beings at all. With their long hair, bird-skin clothing and weather-cankered skin, they looked more beast than human. And after those words –

"Illness."

"Sickness."

– they even ceased to speak to him, or to each other, but stood in the boat like garefowl on an iceberg, simply staring ahead.

Hirta's sandy beach, stripped away by the great storm, had washed ashore again, grain by grain in Village Bay. Farriss was first out of the boat, going over the rail so early that the water came up to his neck. He floundered ashore and set off to run up into the village.

No one was waiting on the beach. Oh, there were a few – the Reverend Buchan, for instance. Murdo, seeing his father, threw up a hand and gave a shout of joy. But Quill, combing the shore for a sight of his parents, could see no one, no one at all. The island boat lay in its usual place. (So it was not damaged or sunk; it could have made the journey out to the Stac to pick up the boys. Given hands to launch it.)

Col Cane called for prayers of thanksgiving. The crew only busied themselves with putting ashore.

"Run the boat onto the beach," said Don.

"We'll not get her off again," the crew responded.

"Oh, the men will all turn to," Don assured them.

The crew glanced at each other and repeated: "We'll not get her off again," and they dropped anchor in the shallows.

A bundle of clothes thrown ashore. And not much of a bundle at that: old clothes so rotten that only the woollens were of use, for unpicking and knitting into stockings. But the bundle of Old Iain's belongings had been enough. The disease must have come in on it.

Smallpox.

One by one, the boys, too, set off to run towards their houses.

The Street itself looked dishevelled and careworn. The great storm that had killed Davie had ripped off turf roofs and smashed chicken coops, strewn The Street with wooden pails and felled a dry-stone wall. Why had no one put things to rights? Re-turfed the roofs? Mended the wall? Why, when the sun was shining, were none of the doors of the cottages open? No women or old men were sitting out on the benches warming their faces and feet.

Boys disappeared inside and reappeared moments later, bewildered or panic-stricken.

The sagging stacks of peat by each house looked sumptuous to boys who had lived without fuel. The greenness of the island dazzled them. The flatness of the ground under their feet felt as if the world had tripped and fallen on its face.

Which indeed it had. Of the twenty-four families who had lived here last year, only a handful of souls remained. The return of the fowling party had just doubled the population.

For an hour, Quill sat in his empty, one-room cottage. The floor was as it had been when he left, strewn with daily sprinklings of peat ash and barley straw and food scraps. *"Needs digging out. You can give me a hand when you get back,"* his father had said. But the strewings were scarcely any deeper than when Quill had gone. They must have died so soon… He would have to start carting the mulch over to the rigs to manure the ground, or nothing would grow in the autumn. No one else to do it now.

He would start tomorrow. Or next week, maybe.

There was a penny brooch on the table, a pair of shoes under it. He would have changed out of his birdskin and sacking, but someone had burned his other suit of clothes for fear they were infected with the pox. He would have washed himself – his ears in particular – but there was no water in the pail. The neighbours must have emptied it scrubbing down the table where the bodies had been laid out before burial. His mother. His father. Who should he thank? Who could tell him the way of his parents' death? There might have been words spoken at the end – messages left for their only son…

The kind of things Davie's mother would want to hear about.

Inside his head, Quill started to concoct what he would tell her, what he would not. But all the pretty lies of a storyteller had deserted him.

A field mouse as big as his fist emerged from the fire grate and sat eating a snail. It was startled to see him, but not afraid enough to run away.

Leaving the door open, to be rid of the staleness, Quill walked up The Street to Davie's house. On the way, he passed Lachlan hurling stones at his own cottage door for the joy of hearing them thud against the wood. "*I'm glad. I'm glad. I'm glad,*" he yelled defiantly, the tears running freely down his face. Quill wondered what kind of misery had existed behind that door for a boy to rejoice at the death of his own parents. Living nine doors apart, how could he have known so little about Lachlan's life? On the Stac, they had been kith and kin to one another... But Quill's mind would not apply itself. Instead, he found himself thinking what a fine raft could be built if he took all those imported wooden doors off the cottages...

He knocked. He knocked again. He hoped that...

And sure enough, his vile wish was granted: Davie's house was empty too. There was no need for Quill to say the unsayable, recount the unbearable, see the mother's face crumple, her heart crumble like dry bread.

In fact there was no need to tell *anyone* that Davie had died on the Stac. Here on Hirta, barely any records had been kept: only "ninety-four dead". Quill found his own parents' graves in the cemetery, but there were plenty of others with no marker, no name daubed in tar. If he and the others kept silent, no outsiders need ever know where or when Davie disappeared from the scene.

But when Davie's dog came in at the open door, and behind him barmy Nettle, sniffing and snuffling, Quill welcomed them with hugs and kisses, and promises of everlasting tenderness and all the food they could eat for ever more.

A steady stream of visitors called at the Manse to ask Reverend Buchan what he knew about their relations – if there was some reason – some *other* reason – why they might not be at home. He told them what they did not want to hear, and promised to pray for them in their hour of grief. Then he praised their fortitude, in the hope they would show some and not collapse in his parlour.

Quill asked if the Reverend knew – if by any chance he recalled – what became of Murdina Galloway, wincing as he asked it, because Murdina had rather disturbed the Reverend's peace and quiet. But the pastor was fulsome in his praise. Murdina's singing and laughter were long since forgiven. For when the smallpox broke out, she had stayed on in Hirta, nursing the sick tirelessly, comforting the dying and the bereaved, and being a veritable mother to all the little orphans. "…Until, of course, she fell ill herself. I cannot tell you precisely when, after that, she died or where she was laid to rest: I was absent with my family by then at the bidding of the Presbytery of Edinburgh.

Poor soul. I was so sad not to be met by her smiling face on my return. You might ask those that the Good Lord has spared in His mercy."

But Quill knew already when Murdina had died. Hadn't he seen the dead garefowl spilling out of its sack? The smallpox might have killed Murdina the summer before, but her wandering spirit had surely been extinguished the day they slaughtered the garefowl on the Stac. After tending the dying on Hirta, her spirit must have flown to the Stac and lodged in the bird, comforting Quill, consoling him, watching over him as bad turned to worse.

"Have everyone gather in the kirk at dusk, Murdo," said the Reverend, mistaking Quill for his friend. "I shall speak words of comfort."

The clapper of the ship's bell presented to the kirk was lying on the ground beside the door, its tongue silenced by too much tolling for funerals. Col Cane said he would mend it. Despite the fact that he was no longer on speaking terms with God (who had left his prayers unanswered), Cane fell back into the role of sexton, tut-tutting over the hastily dug graves, the disorganized overcrowding of the cemetery. He made no mention to Reverend Buchan of his "vigil" on Boreray: the Reverend was a shrewd and educated man and might ask a lot of questions that would be too difficult for a humble man like Col to answer. With luck, the other members of the fowling party would be so devastated with grief over their own losses that they would quite forget the matter of the girl John and his need to requisition the raft. It would not do for his small and scratchy wife (who had survived the smallpox) to get wind of any such scurrilous gossip. Besides, hadn't the Minister himself escaped the troublesome company of his dying flock and gone to Edinburgh?

When the fowlers had left, the door of the kirk had surely been higher than this. The older boys now needed to duck their heads to go inside. When they had left, the barley-straw bales inside had invariably been crowded end to end, so much so that some villagers would be left standing. Now, a half-dozen bales were enough to seat everyone.

Reverend Buchan talked to blank-eyed boys about thanksgiving and joyous reunion. He told them that a heavy responsibility now rested on their young shoulders: to be good men and to secure a future for Hirta.

Meanwhile, Kenneth's sisters sat on either side of him, jabbing him with knitting needles. It had started as a comical way of checking he was real and that they were not dreaming him. It had quickly become a pleasurable pastime, trying to make him curse or yelp in kirk. Quill had never noticed before how much the family members took after each other.

John sat with her mother, but her father was missing. To fetch him back to life, she would willingly have cut her hair and put on boy's clothes for the rest of her life, but instead she was free to be herself and to make her own choices. She decided that Calum, bereft of parents, brothers and sisters, had troubles enough without being reminded of the silly games they had played on the Stac. Games, yes: crab-racing, arm-wrestling, betrothals... He had probably already forgotten his engagement to John.

No one was choosing to remember their time on the Stac. No one was speaking a word about it, and Niall, Keeper of Memories, had nothing in his head these days but a jumble of fantasies.

Domhnall Don sat, back bent, with his elbows on his knees, his hands over his head like a man beneath a rock fall. Stalwart through cold, hunger, fear and provocation, he had shed not a tear on the Stac. Now he rocked forward and back, forward and back and, regardless of who was speaking in the pulpit, repeated over and over "We should never ha' gone. I should never ha' gone." While he looked to the needs of other people's sons, his own family had died, one by one.

Farriss sat with both his daughters in his lap, his wife beside him: a man reborn. As Quill passed by him, he grabbed the boy's arm ferociously tight. "I will bear you up, man, as you bore me up. I swear it." And his little girls smiled at the two dogs Quill had brought into the kirk, then nestled their pock-marked faces against their father's chest.

Quill knew he ought to say how sorry he was about their niece, Murdina Galloway. But there was no speaking the name. People say these things out of politeness, kindness, sympathy – *"we share your sorrow"* – but there were no words to express the depths of Quill's sorrow. If he opened his mouth, the whole kirk might fill up with a million birds and they would all be screaming, like the ones inside his head. He would ask no one about the manner of her death or the whereabouts of her grave. She was gone and nothing would change that.

The Owner's Steward took the opportunity to mount the pulpit and reassure everyone. He made them a solemn promise that the Owner would re-people the island with good workers from Harris and Skye. St Kilda would not want for hands to dig the barley rigs, or fowlers to harvest the birds.

The survivors were supposed to be relieved by the news. Re-people Hirta? Like replacing lost chesspieces so that the Owner could go on playing chess?

Quilliam would not be staying, though. No one could send him new parents or a reason good enough to share his cottage with some family of strangers from Skye. Harris could not replace the Parliament of Elders sitting on their benches in the sun, nor the toddlers interrupting their solemn deliberations. No, Quill's mind was made up. He would leave St Kilda and go somewhere where there were trees, and having seen them, cut them down, so that the birds could never nest there. Perhaps he would build ships from the timber, and sail farther afield. Nowhere could be far enough away. Like the Stac, Kilda was all stone. Fowlers might cling on to its hide like barnacles on a whale, but it neither knew nor cared one jot about them.

"We should never ha' gone away," said Domhnall Don yet again. When the service ended, he was barely aware of the benches emptying around him. He remained seated, hands over his balding crown. Quill stopped beside him and Nettle licked the man, smelling salt.

"It was no' *us* who went," said Quill.

For it was not the fowling party who had gone away. They had been just a few miles across the water, all that time. It was not they who had gone, but everyone else. Their whole world. Quill's whole world.

22

Music and Love

On the Western Isles of Scotland – maybe in other parts, too – the teller of a story must give credit to the storyteller from whom they first heard a tale. So. I who set this down had this story from Quilliam McKinnon of Hirta, and he told it only to me.

None of them talk about what happened on the Stac. A fowling party went after guga. They could not be fetched back for nine months. Most survived. To speak of hardship would be absurd alongside what happened on Hirta while they were gone. So they do not. And anyway, St Kilda men are not a talkative breed. But Quilliam told me.

Most of it he told on the summit of Conachair, the day after I stepped ashore. One boat later, and I might have missed him. But as we arrived from Harris, dear Mr Gilmour set his boat nose-on to the rocks, and the shadow of its mast fell upon the figure of Quilliam McKinnon, waiting there, holding a sack of belongings and two dogs on string leads. In fact he was in such a hurry to board that he lobbed the sack on board straight away: it barely missed my head. Otherwise he might never have troubled to see me.

Now, he looked at me wide-eyed, and gave me the startling news that I was dead. This I strenuously denied, as you can imagine, but he was most insistent.

It is true that I remember nothing of leaving Hirta last summer. I was halfway to my death when Jamie Gilmour's boat sailed up. He threw post and supplies ashore, but hearing the news that all Hirta was in the grips of smallpox, he took nothing on board. No goods. No passengers – said he could not risk carrying contagion to the mainland. There was one thing he took, though. Me.

He's kin to my mother and apparently he had promised her he would bring me home safe and sound. I bless the man, I truly do, for the trouble he took over me.

Before he fled, parents of the fowlers crawled from their sickbeds to beg him: "Fetch home our boys! They're over yonder! Marooned on the Stac! Fetch them home to us!" They were too weak to launch the island boat themselves, you see, and the boat-master – Calum's father, if I remember right – had been the first to die.

But Jamie Gilmour said no, he'd not sail out to the Stac. Don't hate him. He did not say it out of selfishness (though they accused him of it). He said it because he knew their boys were *safer* on the Stac; safe from the disease that was busy killing Hirta men, women and children like summer flies.

When we reached Harris, he quarantined not only me (for fear I infect his family), but himself too, in case he had caught the "plague" from me during the voyage. He must have been watching out for the signs in himself all the while he was nursing me. You would have thought I was his own daughter. I thank God he was spared the pox.

After this self-imposed quarantine, he went to the Owner of Kilda and told him about the boys marooned on the Stac. The Owner said yes, yes, he would send his Steward to take them off. But there were obviously more important things to do. Or maybe the Owner supposed the boys would find their own way home – like stray sheep. Having never visited the place himself, he would not see the problem; the islands and stacs look so close together on a map… In truth, stray sheep would have caused him more concern: sheep are valuable. Boys are two a penny. Maybe he just *forgot* to send help. Happily, when the rents fell due the following summer, he remembered to send his Steward to collect those.

Most people die of smallpox, but not all. The people of Hirta seemed to have little resistance to it, but I am not a Kildan, am I? I pulled through with nothing to show for it but a faceful of scars. And I was able to return. You may wonder that I wanted to. But I had to find out, didn't I? I had to know who had lived and who had died of the smallpox, and whether the dear boys I'd taught their letters had survived their time on the Stac. Not knowing would have killed me, even though the sickness could not.

Up and down, up and down: the prow of the boat sawed up and down on every wave that broke. The man behind me asked impatiently, "Are you getting off, lassie? There's more behind ye, waiting."

The boat was carrying the first of the settlers sent by the Owner to repopulate the island: debtors, poor folk; those who had quarrelled with family; the surplus sons of crofters, wanting their own patch of land to farm... Some people will go anywhere for the sake of a roof over their heads. So I stepped ashore, stumbling a little up against Quilliam, who was only then convinced, I think, that I was flesh and blood.

The desolation of the place was terrible, but its beauty remained just as I remembered it. The silence. Passing clouds snagging on the peaks of Conachair and Oiseval. Shearwaters were making their strange subterranean music, and the graveyard was full of primroses and wild iris. No fine houses. No barns full of plenty. A thousand generations could live here, I swear, and the only riches offered them would be poetry, music and birds. Just maybe, the gift of second sight. I asked Quill what would possess him ever to want to leave such a place, and he asked, "What would possess me to stay?"

"But now you lads are the Lords of the Isles! Who else knows St Kilda like you do? The things you told me! The mysteries! The stories! Without you – what? The Amazon Queen never existed? Nor Fearnach Mor? Nor those Spanish sailors in their poor smashed boat? Nor the Kissing Rock? Because who could ever call them to mind except true Kildans? Without the ones who know these things, all's dead from today. Hirta is writ all over with stories. But without you ones who didna die, no one will ever know them!" And I remember, I brandished a book at him out of my pocket and accidentally hit him on the cheek with it and felt badly because his skin looked sore, and scarred like mine. Still my mouth ran on... "You are the Keepers of the Old Ways...!"

That was when – my lord! – he shot me a look as if I'd called him the Devil-in-tweeds.

"How can I be a Keeper of anything? I couldna keep a stone in a jar!" It was a shout, and the dogs took fright and pulled the string out of his hands and ran off and we were put to chasing them halfway to Ruaival.

So, God forgive me, I told him, "You canna go. Mr Gilmour won't have dogs on his boat. It's a rule with him. I couldna say why, but he'll no carry a dog from hither to yon. He hates 'em." I don't know what possessed me to say such a thing. It had Quill looking at me with those eyes of his and a forward tilt to his body that (I saw later) all the Saved Boys had. It's the same tilt as the Warrior Stac has, as if it's breaching out of the sea the better to breathe.

"But I hav'ta! I promised Davie I'd take care of the dogs!" said Quill. And he started to walk, as if he would walk away from himself if he could. And I walked after, though I had to pick up my skirt hem and run to keep up.

That is when he began to tell his story. I believe it was the first time he had spoken a word of it, and much of it he never spoke of again. We walked to Mullach Sgar and down the Great Glen to Glen Bay then up the back of Mullach Mor, talking. He started with King Gannet and ended with the recent surprise wedding of his friend Murdo to the girl John. Shamefully I was not eager to hear about weddings: my own sweetheart on the mainland changed his mind about our marriage after what the smallpox did to my looks. Revisiting Kilda was my way of putting matters right within me. I needed reminding there were good people in the world.

"A wedding's a wedding," Quill was saying, "but a good piper is the making of it, and Calum played his father's pipes, and it was good – if a touch sorrowful for dancing. We have a saying here: *After the world ends, only music and love will survive.*"

Apparently there is a thing they say, too, at their weddings, over and above the wedding vows. Quill told me it. In fact, he took tight hold of my hand while he did, as if to impress upon me that Kilda men really do have souls. Apparently, for all they resemble birds, they cannot fly. And why is that? Because of the sheer weight of the souls they have to lug about.

"You are the breath I draw, you are the wingbeat of my heart that lifts it high. Your hand keeps me from falling. For you was I born and for you will I live, till Death takes me or the world ends."

I confessed that it was lovely, though a part of me wondered why he was telling me, fixing me like that with those sad eyes of his and telling me those words.

You see, the parts of his story concerning me, he had not told – did not tell till after our wedding a good while later. He still drops them into conversation now and then, as a magpie drops brightnesses in front of his mate, watching me out of the corner of his eye to see if I am offended.

Nothing about Quill can offend me.

Where was I? Ah yes. On the peak of Conachair, watching Jamie Gilmour's boat make ready to sail far below.

"You are staying, so?" he deduced from the fact that I was up here and the boat was down there.

"Till Mr Gilmour calls here next time, yes… But *you* were going."

"I canna, can I? Not without the dogs."

"I lied about the dogs."

He looked at me for the longest time, angry at first and then just bewildered as to why I would do such a thing. Clearly no one on this perfect little island is given to telling lies.

"So *are* you going away, Quilliam?"

"Too late now. When Mr Gilmour calls next time maybe… Oh!"

I believe we remembered both at the same moment.

"*…the baggage!*"

We set off then and there, but with never a chance of reaching the boat before she sailed. The dogs were there ahead of us, but by the time we reached Village Bay, the boat bound for Harris was no more than a white plume on the far ocean. The tides decide these things: you canna say them nay.

Happily, someone had thrown Quill's bundle of belongings ashore again. It lay sagging on the rocks, different colours of cloth peeping out through holes in the hessian.

Not much to show for a life – a bundle of clothes – but some men own less.

And most of what matters, you canna keep in a sack.

Anyway, our life is far from over.

Afterword

St Kilda is a cluster of islands and sea stacs – the most remote in the British Isles. Hirta is the habitable, main island. All the place-names are confusing, their spelling fiendish, and when the sea says you cannot go there, you cannot go.

What you have been reading is a true story…and there again, it's not. Fiction is elastic: it stretches to encircle true facts and then crimps them into shape to create Story. The truth is that a party of eight (not nine) boys and three men went over to Stac an Armin, also known as Warrior Stac, from Hirta and were marooned there for nine months.

They *all* lived – almost impossible to believe, but they did. Only the extraordinarily harsh everyday lives they were already living can have equipped them to survive the ordeal.

Just what they thought and did during that time is lost to history. No one recorded it – only that Hirta was "repopulated" after the epidemic, with new families from elsewhere. When I first heard of the incident, the questions that filled my head were: how did the castaways manage? Whatever did they think had happened back home? What kept them going? What kind of scars did those nine months leave? And yet it is as if no one at the time thought to ask. These were just "fowlers" working for a distant Owner who never visited the remote islands he owned. So long as the bird meat, oil and feathers kept coming, St Kilda was serving its purpose.

The saddest untruth I save till last to correct. When the fowling party was finally brought back to Hirta from the stac, they found not a handful of people still living, but just one.

Two centuries later, in 1930, Hirta was evacuated of its last thirty-six inhabitants at their own request. Many were given jobs (these people from an island without trees) in forestry! The last surviving evacuee, Rachel Gillies, died only recently, aged ninety three.

Now Hirta sits amid the turbulent seas and wild weather, the most remote of places. It still retains its breath-taking beauty, its gloomy entourage of sea stacs, its ancient, mysterious ruins, roofless houses…and doubtless traces of love caught like sheep's wool on the stone walling. They say that "After the world ends, only music and love will survive". But though visitors come and go, there are no residents left there to sing – unless it is the murmuring subterranean puffins, the bleating sheep and the wheeling seabirds overhead.

Birds of St Kilda

GAREFOWL/GREAT AUK

Nearly a metre tall, clumsy and defenceless on land but agile in the water, great auks once lived in vast colonies on rocky islands. Hunted by man, the last in the world was killed in 1844.

ATLANTIC PUFFIN

In flight, these small, pretty auks beat their wings 400 times a minute. They nest in rock crevices or soil burrows and shed their big colourful beaks after the breeding season.

MANX SHEARWATER

Manx shearwaters have been known to live for over fifty years. Often nesting underground, they produce an eerie music.

FULMAR

Gliding, banking and riding the updraughts in front of seaside cliffs, the fulmar is an elegant and stylish flier.

But if threatened, it spits out the oily, smelly contents of its stomach.

GUILLEMOT

These black-and-white birds spend most of their lives at sea. But, on the bird-calendar, they are the first to return to land after winter, sneaking ashore in the pre-dawn dark.

GANNET

Gannets can dive at 100kmph into the sea thanks to nostrils in their mouths, a face and chest "padded" with air pockets, and eyes good at judging distances. Their genus name is *morus*, meaning "stupid", because they are so easy to kill.

GUGA

Gugas are the chicks of gannets. They hatch from big, tough eggs and grow fat and fluffy very fast, then moult. Their meat was once prized as a delicacy.

GREAT BLACKBACKED GULL

Aggressive and powerful, "blackbacks" will launch ferocious attacks on other birds, fish, animals and people. They have a suitably villainous deep "laugh": *kaa-ga-ga*.

STORM PETREL

A kind of fulmar, storm petrels feed at the sea's surface and their seeming ability to walk on water gave them the nickname "St Peters". In storms, they will shelter in the lee of ships. Superstitious sailors imagined they were spirits of cruel sea captains or warnings from "Mother Mary" of oncoming storms.

Glossary

St Kilda Archipelago a cluster of islands and sea stacs north west of Scotland

A chiall mo chridhe my darling

Bauchle awkward lummock of a person; a patched shoe

Bothy a small hut, cottage or – here – place to shelter

Cleit a squat tower built of rocks, capped off with rock, for the drying of birds

Crop a pouch in a bird's gullet where food softens ready to be digested

Escarpment a long, steep slope

Gunwale the rim of an open boat

Obà hush, shh

Kirk a church, especially Scottish Presbyterian

Lee   a place sheltered from the wind

Leviathan   a sea monster in the Bible, usually assumed to be a whale

Manse   the house of a Presbyterian church minister

Meirleach   thief

Merrow   a merman

Plaid   a long piece of chequered or tartan cloth worn over the shoulder

Rigs   family strips of arable land where vegetables and crops were grown

Selkie   a mermaid – seal at sea, woman on land

Stac   a large outcrop of rock rising sheer sided out of the sea

Tinderbox   a box containing tinder, flint and steel used for lighting fires

Wicking   the threading of a wick through an oily bird to turn it into a candle